# LOVE, LOVE, LOVE

# LOVE, LOVE, LOVE
## The "Little Mandate" of
## Catherine de Hueck Doherty

Rev. Robert Wild

ALBA · HOUSE    NEW · YORK

SOCIETY OF ST. PAUL, 2187 VICTORY BLVD., STATEN ISLAND, NEW YORK 10314

*Library of Congress Cataloging-in-Publication Data*

Wild, Robert, 1936 -
    Love, love, love.

        Continues: Journey to the Lonely Christ.
        1. Doherty, Catherine de Hueck, 1900 -
2. Spirituality — Catholic Church — History
of doctrines — 20th century.   3. Catholic
Church — Doctrines — History — 20th century.
I. Title.
        ISBN 0-8189-0549-2
        BX4705.D56W56         1989
        248.4'82                                          88-34243

Designed, printed and bound in the United States of
America by the Fathers and Brothers of the
Society of St. Paul, 2187 Victory Boulevard,
Staten Island, New York 10314, as part of their
communications apostolate.

**Printing Information:**

Current Printing - first digit      2  3  4  5  6  7  8  9  10  11  12

Year of Current Printing - first year shown
   1989      1990      1991      1992      1993      1994      1995      1996

# TABLE OF CONTENTS

[ * * * ]

Introduction .................................... vii

*Chapter One*    Preach the Gospel with your life .  3

*Chapter Two*    Without Compromise .......... 13

*Chapter Three*  Listen to the Spirit
                        — He will lead you .......... 23

*Chapter Four*   Do little things exceedingly
                        well for love of Me .......... 49

*Chapter Five*   Love - Love - Love ............. 71

Note on the Third Volume — A Preview ......... 95

Appendix ...................................... 97

Key To Cited Works ........................... 109

# INTRODUCTION

[ * * * ]

THIS IS the second volume of a proposed trilogy on Catherine Doherty's "Little Mandate," words she received from the Lord during her lifetime and which she considered the essence of her "mandate," her vocation from God. To be understandable the present book presumes some knowledge of Catherine's life. So, for those who may be completely unfamiliar with Catherine, I have decided to include in this Introduction a slight revision of an account of her life I recently wrote for the *New Catholic Encyclopedia*; I thank the editors for permission to reprint it here.

It would be ideal if the reader had read the first volume of this series, *Journey To The Lonely Christ* (Alba House, 1987) though each volume will be understandable as it is. The three volumes will be something like the pictures of a triptych: If you look closely at only one of the pictures, it is complete in itself. But if you stand back and gaze upon all three, you will see how they form one harmonious scene. The three volumes together will form the complete panorama of Catherine Doherty's mandate. Allow me to quote the Little Mandate here, as it will be referred to frequently throughout the text:

Arise — Go! Sell all you possess . . . give it directly,
personally to the poor. Take up My cross (their cross)
and follow Me — going to the poor — being poor —
being one with them — one with Me.

Little — be always little . . . simple — poor — childlike.

Preach the Gospel WITH YOUR LIFE — WITHOUT COM-
PROMISE — listen to the Spirit — He will lead you.

Do little things exceedingly well for love of Me.

Love — love — love, never counting the cost.

Go into the marketplace and stay with Me . . . pray . . .
fast . . . pray always . . . fast.

Be hidden — be a light to your neighbor's feet. Go
without fears into the depth of men's hearts . . . I shall be
with you.

Pray always. I WILL BE YOUR REST.

My first volume treated the first two lines of the
Mandate, "Arise — Go!" and "Little — be always little."
The first line sounds all the major notes of the song of
Catherine's Beloved to her, his will for her: the immense
journey inward to the Beloved's Heart; the dispossession
required to possess him alone; achieving union with the
Beloved through the pain of finding him in the poor.
The immense love of the Beloved impels Catherine to
assuage his thirst for love, to assuage his loneliness
caused by the rejection of Love on the part of so very
many. The Mandate's main thrust is how to achieve
union with Christ in the poor, which is everyone. By
seeking him in the poor, Christ the Good News is revealed to them, and thus His love and loneliness are
assuaged.

Catherine says that the second line — "Little, be always little . . . simple — poor — childlike" — is the most difficult because it concerns "states of being." "What you do," she often said to us, "matters — but not much! What you *are* matters tremendously." On the journey inward to the lonely Christ we are constantly seeking that utter simplicity and perfect interior poverty wherein God is our only Possession.

But I think the heart of the second line is the last description of this interior reality — childlikeness: We have been created to be the children of God ("We are even now the children of God," writes St. John), created to share in God's own nature as much as it is possible for created beings to do so. As far as our own being is concerned, we are seeking to become that original child of God which is our destiny. And so, after sounding the major themes of the Mandate, and, after pointing to the deep states of being out of which we ought to live, the Lord then speaks to her about what to *do*. This is where the present volume begins.

I don't really consider this book a very "creative" work, except perhaps in the sense of arranging the material in some kind of coherent way. There will be many and extensive quotations from Catherine's works. My primary desire is to allow the reader to hear Catherine's song from her own heart. More imaginative, creative presentations of her writings will be the work of the future. In the future people will be relating her spirituality to the contemporary Church, showing its continuity with Russian spirituality, etc. But all this is for the future.

For now, I wish to give people a fairly comprehensive picture of Catherine's Gospel vision from sources that are not yet available to them. It will be sometime yet

before many of the primary sources we have here at
Madonna House will be available for scholarship. In the
meantime, I think I can present the essence of her teaching to the public, and in this way help to guide public
thought concerning the main thrusts of her spirituality.
It is my conviction (I may be wrong but it is my present
conviction) that the research into her writings will con-
firm the main lines traced out in the sources from which I
am presently working.

As in the first volume, I have devised a very simple
reference code which is found in the back of the book.
Many of the sources I use are not published. So I have
kept the references simple. (These references should not
be taken as definitive because when the original sources
are published the references will be different. Unless
otherewise noted, I will be quoting now from original
sources.)

Also, I wish to avoid saying in this and the sub-
sequent volume, "as I said in Volume 1," or "as I will treat
in Volume 3." Any major theme of the Mandate will be
treated somewhere in the three volumes. I hope each
volume speaks sufficiently to your heart so that you will
be moved by the Lord to read the others! There will
be some repetition, because one of the aspects of
Catherine's genius is the intricate weaving of themes in
and out of one another. There is even some danger of
distortion in separating them as I do. But I don't think
there is too much! We Westerners need some order!

Now let me introduce Catherine to those unfamiliar
with her life, or refresh the memories of those already
acquainted with her.

Catherine de Hueck Doherty was the Foundress of
Madonna House Apostolate in Combermere, Ontario,
Canada, and of Friendship House in Canada and the
United States in the 1930's and 1940's. She was born

August 15, 1896, in Nijni-Novgorod (present Gorki), Russia. She died December 14, 1985, in Combermere, Ontario, Canada. A pioneer among the Catholic laity in North America in implementing the social doctrine of the Church, she challenged the Christian conscience of her day by living the radical Gospel of Christ in the face of growing materialism, Communism, secularism, atheism, apathy, and economic injustice.

EARLY YEARS. Her family lived in Ekaterinoslav (Russia), Alexandria (Egypt), India and Paris before finally settling down in St. Petersburg, Russia. Catherine's mother communicated to her an extraordinary faith in the presence of Christ in the poor. In 1912 Catherine married Boris de Hueck. World War I found them both with the 130th Division on the Western Front. As a nurse she was decorated on several occasions for bravery. Escaping to Finland after the 1917 November Revolution, she and Boris ran into Bolshevik sympathizers who almost succeeded in starving them to death. Catherine made a promise to God that if she survived she would give him her life.

CANADA. The couple made their way to Scotland, and then to England, where Catherine was received into the Catholic Church. Raised in the Russian Orthodox Church, Catherine had come to love and understand Catholicism in the convent schools of the Sisters of Sion in both Alexandria and Paris. Thus, God was preparing her to be a bridge between Eastern Christianity and the West. Catherine and Boris emigrated to Canada in 1921. They made their way to Toronto where a son, George, was born to them in July, 1921.

Catherine began receiving invitations to speak about Russia and Communism, eventually joining the

Chatauqua circuit as a lecturer. Such activities brought her again into wealth. But the promise made in Finland would not leave her. She kept hearing the words of the Gospel: "Go, sell all you possess."

Catherine's marriage with Boris had been strained due to the revolution, differing personalities, and a growing divergence in goals. In the early 1930's they separated, eventually obtaining an ecclesiastical annulment (Archdiocese of Montreal, March 18, 1943).

APOSTOLATE TO THE POOR.   In the 1930's the Communist movement began making inroads among the unemployed. Catherine was disturbed. She had vivid memories of what had happened in Russia. Remembering her promise to God, she believed living the Gospel without compromise was the only solution to these social problems. She opened a settlement house in the slum area of Toronto and called it Friendship House. Thus began one of the radical Catholic movements among the poor. Others joined her. They served meals, handed out clothes, and conducted classes in the social teachings of the Church. Under the spiritual guidance of Fr. Paul of Graymoor they formed themselves into a dedicated band with promises and a simple rule of life.

Soon opposition developed: a rumor spread that Catherine herself was a Communist. Misunderstandings also grew on the parochial level. The Archbishop of Toronto supported her but, unable to work in a climate of suspicion, she closed Friendship House. In 1938, however, Catherine accepted a suggestion from Father John La Farge, S.J., that she open a similar Friendship House in Harlem, New York. With the blessing of Patrick Cardinal Hayes, she brought her vision of the Gospel to bear on the racial and social struggles of America.

FRIENDSHIP HOUSE, U.S.A. Catherine's approach was simple: to live the life of the Holy Family of Nazareth among the poor, serving them in small but very basic ways: food, clothes, instruction, love, support. As in Toronto, others were attracted by her life, and dedicated laity formed into a small movement around her. Catherine grew in her ability to form lay apostles into a family of love and service.

In 1943, after the annulment of Catherine's first marriage, she married Eddie Doherty, one of the best-known newspapermen of the time.

Problems also arose in the U.S. Friendship House. There were disagreements about practices and structures. But a deeper rift opened when some members wanted to focus completely on interracial work. Catherine always believed her vocation was much broader, "to restore all things to Christ." At a painful convention in Chicago in 1946, she retained nominal status as Foundress. But on May 17, 1947, she went with Eddie to Combermere in the rural areas of Ontario where the culmination of her life's work was to begin.

MADONNA HOUSE. Through her rich life-experiences, Catherine had gained a faith vision for the restoration of Church and culture at a time when the de-Christianization of the West was almost complete. Not only did she serve the poor and teach the ways of community life to those who joined Madonna House, but she applied her energies and wisdom to liturgical customs, family life, mission outreach, historical museums — in short, to every aspect of human existence.

Before, during, and after Vatican Council II, God urged her on to renew Christ's life in his people. Again, many were attracted to this evangelical community.

xiv          LOVE, LOVE, LOVE

Small mission houses were opened, mostly in North America, but eventually in the West Indies, England, France, and Africa. At present there are 22 missions.

As her own spiritual life matured, she was better able to communicate to the West the treasures of holy Russia. Her spiritual classic, *Poustinia*, is a call to prayer and the "desert" of the heart. *Sobornost* describes a unity in the Holy Spirit beyond any human effort or model. *The People of the Towel and the Water* reveals the Gospel dimensions of the ordinary life.

The Madonna House community numbers about 150 Catholic laymen, laywomen, and priests. There are also about 70 associate priests, and several associate bishops and deacons. It is a Public Association of the Faithful under the Bishop of Pembroke, Ontario. It is, therefore, one Association with three branches, each electing its Director-General by sobornost. Together the three Directors-General govern the whole Apostolate.

CONCLUSION. Even during her lifetime Catherine influenced millions of people and received many awards, among them the Pontifical Medal *Pro Ecclesia et Pontifice* and, in 1977, the Order of Canada, the country's highest civilian honor. Her deep personal life with God, to be found in her diaries and private writings, is still to be made known. She had an extraordinary love for the Church as the radiant Bride of Christ. She insisted that all the baptized were called to fall in love with God and to become icons of his presence in their everyday lives. Many consider her a truly prophetic voice, one of the authentic teachers of the Gospel in the 20th century.

# LOVE, LOVE, LOVE

CHAPTER ONE

# PREACH THE GOSPEL WITH YOUR LIFE

[ * * * ]

THERE IS a real sense in which this phrase — Preach the Gospel — is the heart of the Mandate, since it is the heart of what Jesus told his disciples to do: "Go into all the world and preach the good news to all creation" (Mk 16:15). All the other commands of the Mandate — love, pray, be a light — only achieve their fulfillment if they serve to proclaim the Gospel (in the sense to be shortly explained).

The beginning of the formula for the taking of promises at Madonna House is, "Because I desire with my whole heart to preach the Gospel with my life. . . ." And Catherine wrote to the community once: "I hesitate to say this but the only memorial I wish for myself, humanly speaking, is the growth of the Apostolate in wisdom, grace, and love, so that its members might go forth to the confines of the earth, there to serve God by

preaching the Gospel with their lives and thus restoring
his kingdom" (Begging Letter, January 16, 1963).

*The* service of the Christian to the world, *the* essence
of the Church's mission, *the* way to restore and transform
the world, is precisely by the preaching of the Gospel of
Christ. "Christ loved me," Catherine writes, "in a very
special way because he chose me, with all my weaknesses,
with all my poverty, to preach his Gospel everywhere, at
all times, night and day. For this was I born, to preach the
Gospel by my words, by my very being" (MHWII). "Can
anyone realize the torture, the pain, the sorrow of seeing
so many who do not love him? If you are really in love
with God . . . then you must go, go without resting, to all
the people. You must go to impart the Good News. For
this you have been created. For this you have been
baptized and confirmed . . . that you bring the Good
News to your fellowmen. The Good News must be
preached to the poor. Can you understand this tremendous hunger? It is a hunger for God. It is the kind of
hunger that tears you apart" (U, 12-13).

These themes are constant in her thinking and writ-
ing. Only the Gospel can restore the world to the Father.
*Every word and action* must become an expression of the
Gospel. This is how she can lessen the loneliness of Christ
and return his great love for her. "Woe to me," says St.
Paul, "if I do not preach the Gospel." For Catherine it
would have been a betrayal of love not to preach the
Gospel of her Beloved.

St. Paul also said he only knows one thing — Christ
and him crucified. Some expressions of Orthodoxy (e.g.
Greek) tend to emphasize the risen and glorious Christ.
The resurrection, of course, is central also for Catherine.
But her spirituality is very *Russian* in that she emphasizes

that Christ continues to suffer in his members here on earth. This is a very profound dimension of Russian spirituality, and also a constant desire in Catherine's heart. But what I wish to emphasize in this chapter is that she sees the *preaching of the Gospel* as the goal of everything.

When the poustinik is finally called out of the poustinia, "he moves to the door of his heart because now, faintly yet clearly, he hears the voice of God saying, 'Arise and come into the marketplace and preach the Good News to all you meet.' The poustinik is unsure for a moment or two. He had spent so long . . . in the poustinia. Yet he hears the voice: 'Arise. Come into the marketplace and preach my Gospel with your life' " (St 62).

"Nazareth" forms a very central place in Catherine's spirituality. You might say it is the spiritual atmosphere where we learn what the Gospel is. Living in simplicity with Jesus and Mary and Joseph, we learn of God's tremendous healing love for us. When the Lord left Nazareth he was perfectly ready to preach the Gospel, himself *being the Gospel*. It is otherwise with us. Though we have received the command to preach the Gospel, we ourselves are always in the process of understanding better and better what the Gospel is. Nazareth is where we learn what the Gospel is. However, we cannot wait until we have perfect understanding. One day we must leave Nazareth. The Lord will continue to clarify for us who he is, and what the Gospel is, *even as we journey*.

What does it mean to "preach" the Gospel? In common usage we would say it means *to speak*, to tell others *in words*, about Christ and his message. That is certainly one meaning; but it is not the deepest biblical meaning, nor the meaning that best fits Catherine's understanding.

The words of the Mandate are "Preach the Gospel *with your life*. "Preach," then, has a wider and more profound meaning and significance than only speaking words.

In English, the word closest to the Greek word used for preaching would be "proclaim." And the meaning of "proclaim" can be seen from St. Paul's word about the Eucharist: "Every time you eat this bread and drink this cup you *proclaim* the death of the Lord until he comes" (1 Cor 11:26). And again in 2:1-5, he says his *proclamation* of the Gospel was not with "a display of fine words or wisdom" but rather "with a demonstration of the Spirit and of power, so that your faith might be built not on human wisdom but upon the power of God."

From this we can infer that to "preach" or "proclaim" the Good News is anything — it may be a word, a deed, a miracle, a sacramental ritual — *by which Christ is made present*. The Gospel is Jesus himself, and "preaching him" is any act by which his saving presence is made real and alive. Jesus, walking among the people of Palestine, is the Good News, and not only when he is speaking about the kingdom or his Father's love. Jesus healing the sick is proclaiming the Gospel. Jesus working in Nazareth is proclaiming the Gospel. Jesus suffering silently on the Cross is proclaiming the Gospel.

So, the sense in which I will be using this word, and the sense which best fits Catherine's own use, is this: To preach the Good News, the Gospel, *is making Christ present through our lives, our actions, our words, our whole being*. Because Christ is the Way, the Truth, and the Life, the Love of the Father among us, the only Name by which we can be saved, then the deepest meaning of our life here on earth, the whole purpose of life, is to make him present and known in the world so that all can be saved and come to a knowledge of his truth and love. It is in this context that Catherine's description of the pilgrim is our ultimate goal: "The pilgrim has become, in a sense, a torch. He is light and he is fire. There is no need any more to discuss with him the preaching of the Gospel. He *is* the Gospel! He is fire and light. He is the icon of Christ, *a walking Gospel*" (St 65). "Christians are called to become icons of Christ, to reflect him. We are called to incarnate him in our lives, to clothe our lives with him, so that men can see him, touch him, *in us*, recognize him *in us*" (GWC, 73). In another place she says that Christians must become "the living pages of the Gospel . . . walking catechisms, allowing God to speak, to work, to walk through us" (R, Jan., 1967).

This meaning of "preach" is fundamental to Catherine's vision of the Christian life because she saw the essence of her Mandate as applying the Gospel to every aspect of life, living it out in every possible way, so that Christ could shine forth in as many ways as humanly possible. "Also, I want to remind you that though you get letters from me on every aspect of our spirit . . . actually all can be found in the Gospel of Jesus Christ — if properly read and applied to yourself. For all I do, when all is said and done, is to apply the Gospel of Jesus Christ to the biggest and to the smallest points of our Institute" (SL #58, 1960). "Preach the Gospel. It means that we simply live it. This is our greatest difficulty — to preach the Gospel day in and day out by living, by your speaking, and to believe that this is going to solve things economically, politically, socially, or whatever. Everything is in the Gospel, but we don't want to open our eyes to the tremendous horizon that the simple words of Christ give us. There is nothing, nothing that is not subject to the

Gospel. It is the solution to every problem from now until the parousia" (COLM).

Everything in the world has to be re-created from the foundations up through the Gospel, which is Christ himself. The whole world needs to know and experience the presence of the risen Christ. "The problem is that we Christians do not understand that the world is always hungering for the reality of Christ" (GWC, 73).

Catherine's heart had been won over by the Great Lover whose love has been rejected. What could she do for him to assuage his love and loneliness? The answer is given in this third line: "Make Me and My immense love present to others by living My Gospel in every aspect of life." We might say that the rest of the Mandate is how to make Jesus and his tremendous love present to the world. When two or three are gathered in prayer, he is present. When the Eucharist is celebrated, he is present. When the Gospel is explicitly preached by word, he is present as the Word.

But most central for Catherine — *when you love, Christ is present.*

"Where Love Is, God Is," was the title of one of her earliest books, and it expresses another central core of her Mandate which we will discuss in the fifth line: "Love is needed — much love, whose other name is charity. For where love is, God is; and where God is, there is hope, peace, happiness so hungered for by the multitudes whose diet is one of unrest, uncertainty, fear, and despair" (WLIGI, 35). Whenever we act out of love — serving a cup of tea or listening to someone's sorrows — we make Christ present, we preach the Gospel. By assuaging the lonely Christ we strive to make Christ present in every aspect of life so as to draw people to him.

However, in this chapter, I especially ask the question: "When Catherine preached the Gospel *verbally*, what was the essence of her message?" In season and out of season, she preached *that God is love, and that we must love him back* PASSIONATELY *for all he has done for us.*

> The greatest tragedy of our world is that men do not know that God loves them. The Christian faith, in its essence, is a love affair between God and man. Not just a simple love affair: It is a *passionate love affair.* God so loved man that he created him in his image. God so loved man that he became man himself, died on a cross, was raised from the dead by the Father, ascended into heaven — and all this in order to bring man back to himself, to that heaven which he had lost through his own fault. (GWC, 77)

> How strange that modern Christians seem to miss the greatest point of their faith! The love affair between God and man seems never to have touched the hearts of many religious people. They do not seem to realize that the fulfillment of religion is a return of God's immense love for us. They do not see that the tremendous glad news is that God loved us first. If only they began to love him back passionately, totally, completely, as Christians should, realizing that every word he has said, every commandment he has given, is a commandment of love. It is quite clear that the task of every Christian is to be the leaven of the world by bringing this glorious, wondrous, joyful truth to the hearts of men. Everyone, every baptized person, should go about the world proclaiming this one truth: God loved us first. Let us love him back! Let us learn to obey his commandments and implement his counsels so well that the world and the hearts of men will know, at long last, the peace of the Lord, and will understand and incarnate in their lives

the immense truth that perfect love casts out fears, that it sets men's hearts free and brings joy and gladness into the drabbest existence. To understand that the Christian religion is a love affair between man and God, to begin to love God back passionately as he loved us, this will, if implemented and incarnated in the lives of Christians, also bring peace to our hapless world, and a solution to the seemingly unsolvable problems of our marketplaces. Let us arise and meet the Tremendous Lover before it is too late. (GWC, 77-79)

In thousands of different ways this was the Gospel Catherine preached in words. And by her deeds also she sought to bring this same "glorious, wondrous, joyful truth" to the hearts of everyone.

For Catherine, then, "preach the Gospel with your life" means to *live out the Gospel of God's love in every aspect of life*. Her life is the key to what it meant for her. She *spoke* tirelessly to hundreds of groups all her life. She *wrote* books and articles and literally hundreds of thousands of personal letters. She *gave* food to the hungry and *clothed* the naked. She *listened* to people's problems for thousands of hours, and spent as much time in *counseling*. She *applied* reverence, an interior spirit, and love of the Gospel to every aspect of life and culture — to farming, libraries, kitchens, gift shops, community life — in short, to the whole of human existence. She was constantly asking herself the question, "How does the Gospel apply to this situation? How can I manifest the presence of my Beloved here and now?" Her whole enormous body of teaching is her answer to that question.

Catherine, then, is not an "anonymous Christian." It is not that every time she served a cup of tea she was talking about Christ — but neither would she hesitate to do so! In her words and actions, in her whole life, it was clear that she was a follower of Christ. For her, the call was to manifest Christ *explicitly*. In her mind, a bland humanism with a tinge of the Gospel was not strong enough to counter the waves of darkness in the modern world.

CHAPTER TWO

# WITHOUT COMPROMISE

[ * * * ]

IT HAS OFTEN BEEN SAID that Russians abhor compromise and mediocrity. In their literature, ballet, music, saints, one senses this anguished striving for ultimate perfection — to the breaking point and beyond. Such an *uncompromising striving* to preach the Gospel is a constant dimension of Catherine's teaching and life.

In all my reading about the Russians and Communism I have found no better description of the Russian origins of Catherine's passion than in Bishop Fulton Sheen's *Communism and the Conscience of the West*, Chapter VIII, "Passion," and Chapter IX, "Russia and the Faith." If you can possibly do so, please read them. They are particularly relevant, because much of Catherine's spirit was forged in the furnace of her country's struggle for justice. But, as is well known, the dark forces of Communism took over instead of the light of the Gospel. Just a few excerpts from Bishop Sheen's book.

13

*Speaking of the Western world:*

There is no more Passion, Zeal, Fire, but rather broad-mindedness, which is now considered the greatest of all virtues (160). About the only time we ever hear the word 'passion' is in a movie or a modern novel. But passion was once something real in the world. It was born on the fringes of the Roman Empire, on a hill called Calvary, and on a Friday called Good. That passion was Love, Fire, Enthusiasm. . . . It swept off the world the Greek ideal of moderation and the Roman indifference to the truth (159).

*Speaking of the totalitarian passions of the modern world:*

A passion can be conquered only by a passion; it takes faith to conquer faith; a dogma to match a dogma; a philosophy of life to combat a philosophy of life. At the present time all that we of the Western world have to offer to this new passion is a change in editorial policy . . . (165). Modern Christians have truth but no zeal; materialists have zeal but no truth; they have heat but no light; we have the light but no heat; they have the passion but no ideals; we have the ideals but no passion. Neither of us is perfect. They sin against the Light, we sin against Love. Our crime is our unfulfilled Christian duty, our sprinkling the fires of passion with the cold waters of indifference, our mediocrity which blinds us to the fact that the day of broad-mindedness is over and that all humanity is in search of a soul (167).

It would be difficult to find a more succinct description of a profound dimension and driving force of Catherine's soul: Only a greater passion, dogma, vision, enthusiasm can combat, not only Communism, but all

the other isms less than the Gospel. Our answer is the
Gospel of Christ. If it was truly lived by all Christians, we
could change the whole world. Having personally experienced her Russian people passionately striving to
remake the whole world by following the Antichrist, she
was determined to be *just as passionate* in restoring everything to Christ.

There is a remarkable document from 19th century
Russia called "the Revolutionary Catechism" written by
Nechayev, one of the first social nihilists. It is a powerful
expression of this anarchist, revolutionary passion of the
modern Russian soul turned in the wrong direction:

1.   The revolutionary is a doomed man. He has no
personal interests, no business affairs, no emotions, no
attachments, no property and no name. Everything in
him is wholly absorbed in the single thought and the
single passion for revolution.

2.   The revolutionary knows that in the depths of
his being, not only in words but in deeds, he has broken
all bonds which tie him to the social order and the
civilized world.

3.   The revolutionary despises all doctrine . . . he
knows only one science: the science of destruction.

4.   For the revolutionary, everything is moral
which contributes to the triumph of the revolution.

5.   All the gentle and enervating sentiments of kin-
ship, love, friendship, gratitude and even honor must be
suppressed in him and give place to the cold and single-
minded passion for revolution.

GOAL:   To weld the people into one single uncon-
querable and all-destructive force — this is our aim, our
conspiracy, our task. (In Robert Payne's *The Life of Lenin*).

Yes, "to weld the people into one single unconquer-
able force," this is *our goal* also, Christ's goal; but we call it

the Mystical Body of Christ, the Kingdom of God, the Church. To hear, on tape, Catherine's prophetic talk, "The Spirit of the Madonna House Apostolate" (the text of which I included in *Journey*) is to hear the passion of a Russian Christian revolutionary — a revolutionary for Christ. She said there:

> We are passionately, utterly, completely, in love with God, or should be, as we progress along this road of our Apostolate. We breathe, we live, we eat, we sleep, only for one reason: To serve him whom our hearts love, and to extend his kingdom. Unless our hearts are filled with the charity of Christ, and we burn with the zeal of this charity, we are like sounding brass and tinkling cymbals. Without love, nothing that we do will matter. No restoration will follow. Our activities will only be extensions of things Communists and pagans do. The difference between us and them is motivation. We do these things because we cannot help doing them, because, like a people on fire, we must serve; otherwise our love for God will simply tear us apart! And so that is our vocation — to burn, to die, to become a flame, so as to make room for Christ to grow in us. You have no past, no future. You have no mother, no father. You have no wife, no husband. You have no children, no relatives. You are alone, facing your Lover, God. No one and nothing is between you and God. (SMHA)

It's powerful even to read, isn't it! (You should have heard her speak it!) It's the same, total, uncompromising spirit as Nechayev's, only turned to the light instead of to the darkness.

"Without compromise," for Catherine, means *passion*! It is not an exclusive prerogative of the Russian soul, but they seem to have a generous share of it! Its ultimate *Christian* source is to be found in an awareness of what Christ has done for us. In this sense it is a quality of all the saints. To really understand the essence of the Gospel is to be passionately in love with God, to return love for love. "What does it mean to love God 'infinitely'?" the child Catherine once asked her mother. "It means to love God without measure," was the reply. That is what Catherine tried to do.

Catherine was aware of how she herself failed to reach this ideal. If she was sitting at a table and challenged about not living up to what she was preaching, she would say (and we who knew her saw her say and do this many times): "Do you see this table? This is the whole Gospel I try to preach." Then drawing a little square with her finger in one of the corners of the table, "Do you see this little square? That is what I do." But she insisted that the whole Gospel had to be preached.

There is a perennial temptation among Christians only to preach what they are doing, or what they are capable of, considering it "insincere" if they preach something they themselves are not living. Catherine did not believe that. The command is to go out and preach the *Gospel*, not preach "where you're at" in your own life and struggle with the Gospel. People do not want to hear where you're at! Of course, we must strive to live the Gospel; and, no doubt, the more we live it the greater power our words will have. But one of the agonies of being a preacher of the Gospel — of being a Christian — is that we must preach and witness to a message beyond us, a message not our own, a message we ourselves are conscious of not fully living up to.

The Gospel response to God's love is to love him back with one's whole heart, mind, soul. This absolute response also must be preached. Yes, it is impossible. But the Gospel reveals the grandeur of what our hearts are capable of. Our hearts have been made for God, and with God's help we are capable of loving him with great passion and generosity. Catherine believed that *people must be called to this great and passionate love.*

The following quotes, although all from the same book (*The Gospel Without Compromise*) were actually written over a very long period (since the book is a collection of her editorials over the years). This passion, intensity and uncompromising striving was part of her Russian Christian soul, and present in all she said and did.

> Yes, we Christians must make our decisions for or against Christ. He said, 'Who is not with Me is against Me.' He demands total allegiance, total surrender, total acceptance of his Gospel, total love (75).

> The answer is that we must begin to live the Gospel without compromise. We must be ready to lay down our lives for our fellow man. Lay our life down also for the incarnation of the Good News if we want Christ to be known to others. There can be no half-hearted following of him. It is all or nothing!

> Humanity today is a man who must touch the wounds of Christ in order to believe. . . . the only way to show these wounds of Christ to others is to *live the Gospel without compromise. Does that mean that we must turn our lives upsidedown? Does it mean a complete change of values? Does it mean the breaking up, the demolition of our comfortable way of life? Quite simply, yes, it does!* (74).

> The Gospel can be summed up by saying that it is the tremendous, tender, compassionate, gentle, extraordinary, explosive, revolutionary law of Christ's love. He calls each one of us who calls himself a Christian. He calls us directly. There is no compromise in his call. We

can find umpteen quotations in the Gospel that will vividly bring forth to our minds and hearts how simply and how insistently he calls us to be like him, and to accept his law of love without compromise. His call is revolutionary, there is no denying it (71).

His commandments mean risk, great risk. . . . God offers us risk, danger, and a strange insecurity that leads to perfect security. . . . It is a tremendous risk because we must also love our enemies. . . . As this involvement of love among brothers grows and deepens, we enter into a *revolution*. A revolution in which there is violence directed only against oneself (71).

I wonder how long we can sit on the fence of compromise. God is not mocked. Christians must openly declare their allegiance to Christ, or their non-allegiance to him. The story of the disciples who had to choose is repeating itself today among us. 'Who do you say that I am?' It is time . . . we stopped fooling around. If ever there was a time when humanity needed followers of Christ and fewer fence-sitters, that time is now (75).

Why then do we not try the way of love, the way of the Gospel? Why do we not apply the Gospel without compromise to our personal, national, and international life? Why do we not live by his law of love? What is stopping us? (76).

In our own day (and perhaps in every age) the "revolutionary" dimension of Christ's love is always in danger of being misdirected. Again, Bishop Sheen says it well:

Modern youth wants what Europe wanted at the close of the last war — Passion, fire, enthusiasm. It too wants to

believe that there is evil in the world, and that a man
ought to fight against it. But unfortunately, both the
capitalists and the Communists have convinced them
that the only evil is in the economic order. As a result the
Communists believe it is possible to combine a passion
for social justice with a complete unconcern for individual righteousness. They have a social conscience to
right the wrong of others but no individual conscience
to right their own; they organize to combat the alleged
wickedness of others, but dispense themselves from all
personal obligation to morality, conscience and God. As
long as they fight for the underprivileged they feel
privileged to do all the wrong. Thus does youth feel a
merciless aggression against wrong which fills up the
void made by the loss of the Grand Passion of Love, but
which only increases the world's disorder, for now their
fires burn their neighbors' houses and not the dross of
their own hearts (164).

Catherine's whole spirituality is concerned, first of
all and always foremost, with channeling the "Grand
Passion of Love" inward, towards the human heart. She
believes, of course, that the Gospel must permeate the
whole of society. But it permeates first of all by passing
through the transformed heart of each person. When
this person has been transformed by Christ, then he or
she will have new eyes and a new heart both to see clearly
how to go about the task of restoration, and have the
strength to do so. Until we ourselves are transformed, we
will not be able to see how to make Christ present to the
world. We will only be making ourselves present — which
is the whole problem!

But the radiant, interior fire enkindled through this
conflagration of the human dross *within ourselves* will
make Christ present in the world only if we love him
*passionately, without compromise*. Only then will his light

be able to dispel the terrible darkness. A half-hearted, mediocre love will only bring him to the world in a mediocre way.

## Preach the Gospel

Another meaning of the phrase "without compromise" in reference to the Mandate in Catherine's life was the call to preach the *whole* Gospel, the authentic Gospel, and not a watered-down version of it. Often when Catherine taught in the dining room a profound silence would follow. She was often upset by this, and wondered why there wasn't any feed-back or comments or *something*. My own experience (which I'm sure was that of many) was that what she said just struck one as absolutely true — Gospel *true*. It was all there — complete, challenging, demanding, true to what Jesus taught. What was there to say?

To sum up, then, the two phrases of this third line: Christ is the Light and transforming Love of the world. Our call is to preach him, that is, to make him present. He is made present — preached — by faithfully speaking and living the words of the Gospel. God has loved us infinitely by sending us his own Son. As impossible as it may seem, we are called to love God in return with our whole being — with an uncompromising passion and intensity. And it is primarily *love* (the subject of the fifth line) which makes Christ present.

CHAPTER THREE

# LISTEN TO THE SPIRIT — HE WILL LEAD YOU

[ * * * ]

NICHOLAS BERDYAEV was one of the greatest and most influential of the modern emigre Russian thinkers. He flirted with Marxism for a brief period. But then, the reorientation of his thinking towards Christianity made him very unwelcome in the new Soviet Union. He was exiled, never to return. Already in the 1920's Catherine was reading his works; she had an opportunity to meet him in Paris on one occasion.

I would like to begin this section on the Holy Spirit in Catherine's thinking with a passage from the very conclusion of Berdyaev's book, *The Fate of Modern Man*:

The hour has struck, when after terrible struggle, after an unprecedented de-Christianization of the world, and its passage through all the results of that process, Christianity will be revealed in its pure form. Then it will be clear what Christianity stands for, and what it stands against. Christianity will again become the only and final refuge of man. And when the purifying process is finished, it will be seen that Christianity stands for man and for humanity, for the value and dignity of personality, for freedom, for social justice, for the brotherhood of men and nations, for enlightenment, for the creation of a totally new life. And it will be clear that *only* Christianity stands for these things. The judgment upon Christianity is really the judgment of the betrayal of Christianity, upon its distortion and defilement; and the justice of this is that of judgment upon the fallen world and its sinful history. But the true and final renaissance will probably begin in the world only after the elementary everyday problems of human existence are solved for all peoples and nations, after bitter human need and the economic slavery of man has been finally conquered. Only then may we expect a new and more powerful revelation of the Holy Spirit in the world.

One of Berdyaev's themes is that, eventually, all the modern "isms" and ideologies will prove bankrupt — Communism included. The Russians, because of their uncompromising nature, have presented to the world what absolute atheism and materialism look like. I believe that Catherine, in her life and teaching, has presented to the world what the absolute choice for the *Gospel* looks like. For both Berdyaev and Catherine, the Holy Spirit is meant to be the inspiration for a whole new order of civilization. Everything must be re-created from the bottom up — economics, politics, all of culture.

The Mandate which the Lord gave to Catherine was to prepare for a *new order of the world* under the inspiration of the Holy Spirit of Jesus. But Catherine was not going to wait for some stage of justice to be fulfilled before the Spirit's coming. I think it is part of the Gospel vision that the Kingdom grows within the confusion of the world. We do not wait for some prior stage of development. Christians begin to live *now* the absolute demands of the Kingdom.

## The Spirit As Love Between The Father And The Son

The obvious meaning of this line of the Mandate — "Listen to the Spirit" — is the Holy Spirit as the *Guide* along our pilgrim way. He is the One who conducts us along our journey inward to the lonely Christ and into the heart of the poor. He is all this and much more for Catherine, as we shall see shortly. But first and foremost, the Spirit *is love itself, that passionate, immense, all-embracing Love* which we spoke about in the first chapter. If uncompromising love is the answer to the world, it is *the Holy Spirit himself who is this Love.*

For Catherine, the life of the Blessed Trinity is always *the deepest reality in her consciousness.* We have come from the heart of the Trinity, and we shall return there. All life should become a reflection of the life within the Godhead. So, when she began to speak, on one occasion, about the Holy Spirit, her thoughts first turned to who the Spirit was in the life of the Trinity:

Who is he, this Holy Spirit? Pause for a minute. Try to shut out all the noises within and outside of you. Try with his grace to catch a tiny glimpse of the intensity of the love of the Father for the Son and the Son for the Father. So awesome, incomprehensible and passionate is the love of the Father and the Son for one another that it becomes visible, as it were, and begets the Third

Person of the Most Holy Trinity, the Spirit of fire, the Spirit of love. Why does he come to us? He comes every moment of our lives to help us to become saints, lovers of God, for he is the Sanctifier.

Just as the Lord prayed that we might be one as he and his Father are one, so he desires that we love God and one another as passionately and intensely as he loves the Father. This Love is a Person, the Holy Spirit, and he has been given to us to become saints, that is, lovers of God and one another, since He is Love itself.

## Spirit — Love Creator

It is often Catherine's poetry which gives most eloquent expression to the inexpressible. Here are sections of a poetic meditation on the ineffable mission of the Holy Spirit. First she speaks about creation itself, both of the world and the human person:

Fire, Flame, and mighty Wind together shape and reshape creation, renewing the face of the earth. But, oh, the sight of the might that descends on the soul of man. The wind lifting up, the Fire begetting a flame; and then lighting a fire again in the soul of man. Such is creation — Love its foundation. Love is a Fire, Love is a Flame, Love is a Wind, possessing, enticing, calling the soul of man. Sparks of the Fire falling light the universe; they are descending. Grace is a spark, grace is a gift of Flame and of Fire. Shower of love, falling, descending into the soul of man. Mystery profound, adorable, incomprehensible, lovable to the soul of man.

Next, miracle of miracles, the Spirit of Love fashions the *Incarnate One*:

> Spirit uncreated, descending, incarnating the unencompassable, becoming encompassable, touchable, feelable — Word made flesh, walking the earth, sharing Flame and Fire, touching with strange desire the soul of man.

Then, Love Incarnate dying for us:

> Loving, loving, spilling love like a flame on the earth, dying of love on a cross for the soul of man. Then descending into death's domain, returning unscathed, for what power does death have over Fire, Flame and Wind? Returning, ascending, only to send more Fire, more Flame to light the path of the soul of man.

Then the continuing work of the Spirit in the world after Christ's return to the Father, "to keep intact the memory":

> To keep intact the memory of the Man Who was God. Spend-thrift of love, Pauper and King, Ragman desirous, desirous of buying raggety souls as long as they are souls of men. For the Wind will embrace, and the Fire and Flame will efface, and the Fire renew the soul of man, lifting, lifting, lifting it up again into the hands of him from Whom Wind, Fire, and Flame descended, God the Father unseen and unknown. Oh, the mystery of Love uncreated! Rise and come! The Wind is nigh. The Crimson Dove will lift you up into the heart of the King, and he will bring you before the face of the Father, so full of grace. Rise, O soul, this is the hour. The Wind is nigh. Come! for this you were created, O soul of man. To know the feel of the mighty Wind. Listen! To nestle

in the arms of the Crimson Dove, to be lifted above, above, right into the arms of the Bridegroom. Rise, O soul of man! This is the hour, this is the time to know ecstasy divine!

In this one poem Catherine has expressed the heart of who the Holy Spirit is (ad extra, outside the trinitarian life, as the theologians would say) — Love Itself who has fashioned creation, the Incarnation and now is the ever-burning flame Who "lights our path" into the arms of the Beloved, who "keeps intact his memory." All the other aspects of the Spirit's activity have this as final goal: "Here is the Wind. Let yourself go. Enter the Fire, become a flame. This is the time to fall in love again. The Bridegroom waits. Enter the Wind. Be lifted up into the arms of the King, O soul of man."

As St. Paul says, "The love of God has been poured into our hearts through the Holy Spirit who has been given to us." It is by being open to the Holy Spirit's action within us that we are able to live — be — the uncompromising love to which the Gospel calls us. "To burn, to die, to become a flame — this is our vocation," Catherine had often told us. How can we do this? By being open to the Holy Spirit who is the very Love of the Father for the Son. "It is to love, to burn that we have come together. And Who brought us? The Fire of Love, the Holy Spirit. Little flames, coming together, each growing, uniting in various patterns. . . ." (SMHA).

## Listen To The Spirit

The above reflections give the proper setting to Catherine's specific intuitions about the Spirit in the

Mandate. We now proceed to the more specific meanings of this line.

We have a remarkable tape by Catherine entitled "How the Little Mandate Came to Be." In it she reveals how the Lord fashioned within her the particular vision of the Gospel he wished her to follow and teach to others. For that is what a spirituality is — a particular vision of the Gospel for a particular time in history. The following passage, from Catherine's own recollections, will lead us into the heart of this line of the Mandate. In the following passage she was struggling to understand what it meant to preach and live the Gospel without compromise:

I prayed, but nothing very much happened. One night I was sitting at home. We had a fireplace. It was late and . . . I was lying before a fireplace, very much like in Russia — but this time very much alive and not at all asleep and not hungry, except for knowledge. In this case, the type of knowledge that I cannot get through books but that I so often talk about and which arouses ire in so many people because I speak so much about it; but I always believed that if you really want to know something about God's will, God, or a mystery of the faith, you have to be passive, and you have to pray very simply, ask God, and it will come. So I was lying before this fireplace, very quietly, perhaps praying to God, asking him to explain to me why I started using this phrase 'preach the Gospel with your life without compromise,' especially the part, 'with your life.' What did it mean? It bothered me. Everything bothered me at that time. Everything seemed supernatural, natural, crazy hallucinations — from the devil, from God. I was praying in faith . . . and at that moment a thought came. Now don't ask me if it was my thought, my own explanation,

my own intellect. I didn't hear a word. I didn't do anything. I was just lying there. I asked a question and if
you wish to put it spiritually . . . in the passivity of the
Spirit I was waiting for an answer, for the Gospel said,
'Ask and you shall receive.' I wasn't sure that I would
receive it that night, but I was sure if I continued asking,
sooner or later, I would receive it. Because I asked in the
name of Jesus Christ. So, ergo, the Father had at some
time or other to answer it, through his Son, or the
Mother of the Son, or the Holy Spirit; he had to answer
in *some* way.

Then a thought came, clear as crystal: 'Listen to the
Spirit, He will lead you.' Now, to a Russian, that's a
perfect answer! I asked myself, 'Why didn't I think of
that before?' But then I stopped thinking, for when
such answers come it's best to fold the wings of one's
intellect and accept it and rejoice and glorify
God.   (HMCB)

In the context, then, of the spirituality of the Mandate, the phrase "Listen to the Spirit" came in response
to her request, "What does it mean to preach the Gospel
without compromise?" or, "What is the Gospel, how does
one live the Gospel?"

In the Gospel the Lord said that one of the main
missions of the Spirit would be to help us understand
what he, the Lord Jesus, had taught us: "He will bring to
your minds everything I have told you." In Catherine's
writings, then, there is a great deal of emphasis on the
Holy Spirit as a Source of light, helping her to understand how to live out the Gospel: "Suddenly, through the
goodness of the Father, we're given the Spirit; and He
enters into our apostolate with a song, with words, the
words of the Father that came to us through the Son. He

[the Spirit] has the capacity to crack those words open and to make what is intolerable pleasurable"   (TOLM).

In both Latin and Greek the biblical word "obey" means to listen intently, or better, to "hear intently." And the biblical meaning of "hear" is not like hearing or listening to music. It means *doing what you hear*: "Blessed are those who hear the word of God and keep it." When a real servant hears a command there is no interval between the hearing and the doing: they flow together into one action. "I tell my servant go and he goes," said the centurion to Jesus.

For believers, true knowledge comes from obeying God, doing the Word. If we do what God asks, then we will understand. So the answer that Catherine received was this: "Obey — do — the Spirit's leadings, and then you will understand the Gospel." *It was mostly by her concrete incarnation of the Gospel, step by step, that God taught her what the Gospel was. By doing the Gospel the Spirit taught her what it was.*

> Listen, listen with your hearts, with your souls, listen with an ear attuned, listen with expectation, desire, and love. And you will hear the coming of the wind of the Holy Spirit, mightier than any tornado that ever hit the earth, with the speed that cannot be counted or computed by any machine or mind of man; and yet, gentle as the evening breeze, swift, immense, fast, harmless to nature and to man, nay, on the contrary, leaving in His passage light and warmth, peace and wisdom, fortitude and long-suffering, charity, faith, hope and all the gifts and virtues.   (SL #102, 1962)

It's at the very heart of our belief in revealed religion — throughout the Old Testament (especially in the prophets) culminating in *the* Prophet, our Lord Jesus

Christ, God's Word in the flesh — that God *can and does* speak to us: "Thus says the Lord. . . ." And this Word of the Lord is the light of our life: "Your word is a lamp for my feet and a light for my eyes."

Now, the ability to hear the Word of God, to hear what God is actually saying, is itself a gift from God. We need the Spirit of God to hear and understand the Word of God. You might say that the desired fruit of the deep "states of being" which are in the second line of the Mandate — littleness, simplicity, spiritual poverty, and especially childlikeness — is to dispose us to hear the Word of God. For it is this Word by which we live — we live by every word that comes from the mouth of God. To be able to hear this word, in the biblical sense of responding to it, is our very life; especially the Word of Jesus in the Gospel.

So, the stripping that we go through, the kenosis, is to dispose us to become teachable, docile, to the voice of the Holy Spirit. This is what one of the traditional titles for the Holy Spirit, Father of the poor, means for Catherine: He is the One who creates *emptiness within us so we can be filled with God's riches:*

*Pentecost — 1969*

This is the time of emptiness. The time of shedding whatever clings to my heart, my soul, my mind, my hands! This is the time of standing so very still, allowing God to shape me to his will, to shape me finally indeed into the shape in which he wants me to appear before the Father! This is the time of nakedness, being prepared for pilgrim's garb, and the becoming truly a pilgrim of the Absolute, who stands ready equipped,

ready to go into the mapless land of faith! This is the
time of listening with heart and soul, of total folding of
the wings of the intellect, to hear the Spirit speak! For
this is the hour of Wind and Fire that will burn the dross
in me, the Wind and the Fire that will lift me to
him!   (JI, I)

Father of the Poor, of whom we are the poorest. He
comes to make us rich. Do not be discouraged when we
speak to you of being poor. Rejoice! When we speak
about our poverty, we speak theologically. While we
creatures of God are poor because we have nothing of
our own, at the same time we are rich because we are
created in the image and likeness of God; and we are
rich above all because God loves us. Thus we are both
poor and rich, but we certainly need the Father of the
Poor to make us see how rich we are. So he comes.
(SL #102, 1962)


## "Folding The Wings Of The Intellect"

In the passage I quoted above, where Catherine was
praying for light as to the meaning of living the Gospel
without compromise, she said she was hungry for
knowledge, "the type of knowledge that I cannot get
through books but that I so often talk about and arouses
ire in so many people." At the end of that same quotation
she explains: "Then I stopped thinking, for when such
answers come it's best to fold the wings of one's intellect
and accept it and rejoice and glorify God." And in the
poem "Pentecost — 1969," quoted above, there is the
line, "the total folding of the wings of the intellect to hear
the Spirit speak." Another phrase which, for our
purposes here can be used synonymously with "folding

the wings of the intellect," is "putting your head in your heart." Catherine often used these phrases, and they often *did* cause ire, confusion, and misunderstanding! This is the place to briefly say something about this aspect of her teaching, for it deeply concerns the meaning of "Listen to the Spirit."

These phrases, for Catherine, are her *symbolic ways of describing how true knowledge is acquired.* And what is true knowledge? Wisdom.

> During a discussion about the Holy Spirit someone asked me what wisdom is. For a moment I was lost for an answer, but the answer is so simple that I was astonished that anyone should ask. Wisdom is the simplicity of love. He who really loves God, and others as they should be loved, is wise! He is not wise with his own wisdom, but with the wisdom of God who always comes to dwell in a soul which has so died to itself that it offers him space to dwell in. If God dwells in you and acts in you, how can you fail to be wise? To acquire wisdom, all you have to do is die to self. (SL #102, 1962)

Passionate, uncompromising love is the healing and light of the world. To know how to love in the simplicity of a child of God is itself a gift of God; it is true wisdom. This light flows from kenosis, from self-emptying, which the Spirit effects in us as a result of the carrying of our cross every day and following Jesus.

These phrases often aroused such "ire" in people because they were understood in an anti-intellectual sense. Nothing could be farther from Catherine's intention. In 1962, in a letter to the community, she explained her meaning very clearly.

She said she was often criticized for being against Degrees and academics: "She functions on a somewhat

emotional level of 'caritas only.' " When she went into the
slums to serve the poor she didn't have time for much
intellectual study. It was only years later, she tells us, that
"I understood that I had been put through the highest
school of learning, GOD'S SCHOOL OF LOVE. It was then I
began to understand that if we give up our intellect to
God — at his request — he will return it to us cleansed of
all that is not him. And our secular and spiritual
knowledge will be made new and powerful in him."
(SL #113, 1962)

People must be able to lay aside intellectual pursuits
for humble tasks which demand love, detachment from
self, and humility.

> When filled with this love and detachment and holy
> indifference, when they truly *mean their fiat, then their
> learning time has come.* They will never make the mistake
> of thinking that intellectual and professional
> knowledge are pass-keys to human hearts. They will
> know that only *love* is important. In understanding this
> they will become wise with the wisdom of God . . . all the
> rest will be added unto them. To me one has to first *be*
> before the Lord, and for this one has to go to Nazareth.
> Then one has to *do* for the Lord. After that one can go to
> any school that will make the works of the Lord shine
> more clearly.    (*ibid.*)

Thus, there are two basic aspects to Catherine's posi-
tion about the use of the intellect. First, there is a kind of
knowledge that is from God, from the Holy Spirit, that
cannot be acquired from study. It is wisdom, how to love.
Secondly, all knowledge must be subject to God, subject
to the light of faith, and used for God's honor and glory.

Before she went to school her father prayed this
blessing over her: "May the Holy Spirit overshadow you,

child, so that your mind may be opened to all useful knowledge . . . so that you may understand that all knowledge must be used for the glory of God and the service of our fellow man."

One of the catastrophic fissures in Western civilization is the separation of the mind from its dependence on the light of faith. Traditionally, in the West, revelation was seen as the highest form of knowledge, and philosophy, or whatever human reason could discover, was seen as subject to the light of faith. One thing Catherine seeks to restore is this proper order in the use of the mind. She is not against the intellectual life:

> I don't know how many times I have to repeat it but I NEVER DENIED THE INTELLECT AND ITS POWER. I also want to go on record that . . . as long as I live, and I hope my successors will continue this accent . . . I want to pass on the vision of giving the staff workers of Madonna House *the benefit of all possible intellectual culture . . . whatever is needed to restore the whole man in Christ. Nevertheless, I will also never cease to explain, clarify, pray, that the members of our apostolate — the higher they go on the scale of intellectual and spiritual values — the better they will understand that they will have to 'fold the wings of their intellect' and become like little children, open of heart and soul and mind to the Holy Spirit who alone can lead them (with the help of his blessed spouse, the Blessed Virgin), to a true encounter with Christ and, hence, with the Father! This type of knowledge is beyond man's intellect! Yes, beyond his natural, human intellect — but not beyond his divine, supernatural self. Christ desires this encounter with himself but he demands a child-like, humble heart.* (SL #179, 1965)

Catherine wants to make it clear that the most important kind of knowledge — wisdom, how to love —

comes from God, and child-like, humble, self-emptying dispositions of the soul are essential to receive this knowledge:

> I constantly stress the 'workings of God on the soul and the need of the soul to be open and passive or receptive to those workings of his grace.' I constantly stress that a true encounter with God . . . really happens when God acts upon us in the special manner that he alone can act, and gives us a knowledge of himself through the Holy Spirit. *This knowledge is beyond our intellect, beyond our capacity to acquire. It is a pure grace, a pure gift of love from him to us.* (*ibid.*)

Perhaps the passage in *Poustinia* where she asks the rhetorical question "Can the poustinik study?" best sums up her thinking on this subject.

"What do they mean by the word 'study'? Study God? Impossible. His chief study must be to ask the Lord, 'Please teach me about yourself.' " In keeping with our spiritual traditions, both East and West, Catherine simply insists that there is a kind of knowledge which only God can give us. Her emphatic and constant admonition, "fold the wings of the intellect," is meant as a strong antidote to our Western hubris which really does believe that *all* knowledge comes from study and the unaided human intellect. Catherine keeps turning people to learn directly from the Holy Spirit.

But this does not mean that everything must be learned in this way. She values study and learning very highly. When can one study then?

She describes the poustinik (who can be taken here as a person growing in faith) walking through the desert; he keeps coming to small water holes. In each water hole is the water of faith; and faith begins to grow as the poustinik drinks more and more. He understands that this assuaging of his thirst is a gift from God and not from his own understanding.

> . . . You suddenly arrive at a beautiful river. You come to the edge of it and know that you can drink from it until you die. Now faith has taken hold of you and nothing, nothing, nothing can separate you from the river. You realize that through your journey you have fallen in love with God, and that it was really his face you saw in each water hole. The water holes were God's gift of faith to you, for God alone could quench your thirst. *When the poustinik has arrived at this river of faith, then he can study. Then he will never be misled by what he studies.* (P 102-103).

In many of today's universities, how often it happens that people with weak faith lose their faith when they begin to seriously study. We have met so many young people at Madonna House to whom this has happened. Their faith was weak when they entered college, so a new and powerful stream of knowledge subverted the true order of knowing.

Catherine desires that people drink deeply of the river of faith *first*; and then, whatever they study will always be subject to the superior light of faith. And also, one must realize that the truly superior knowledge — of faith and how to love — are always *gifts of the Holy Spirit.* She is for the true "liberation of the intellect" (SL #179) where the infused knowledge from God orders and gives true illumination to whatever we know and learn.

## Listening

One of Catherine's words from poustinia (P 157-162) was listening. And because in this sharing she spoke not only about listening to God but also about listening to oneself and to others, this "listening" has a slightly different meaning than the "listen/hear/obey" of the scriptural word which we have been discussing. This second meaning is important because many of our recent mission houses are called "prayer/listening" houses. It means, of course, to obey the Holy Spirit, but it has other connotations. This kind of listening is a most significant aspect of our vocation.

## Listening To God

"It is an interiorized situation in which he comes to you and clears a little bit of your heart. He makes it comfortable there for himself; and there he talks to you as a Friend to a friend. You feel as if you are sitting at his feet like Mary, listening, just listening."

Here the listening takes on the quality of simply "being with." You are attentive with your whole being to your Friend, the Lord. He is not necessarily telling you to do something; he is enjoying your presence and attracting you to enjoy his. You might say it is a "contemplative listening" and presence of One to the other. And in this atmosphere you come to the Trinity.

What does it mean to come to the Trinity? To me it means to come into the light from a very great darkness. It means to come into peace from great turmoil. It means to come into joy from a painful and joyless

journey. It means I realized that I had to love myself
more than I did because God loved me. I grew in reverence, love, and adoration of the God who created me
and dwelt within me. I saw that I was an heir to my
Father's love and to all his goods. I realized in depth that
I was an icon of Christ. I saw that I was a sister to Christ,
and that I indeed always walked in the shadow of the
wings of the Holy Spirit.   (P 160)

There is a listening to God where one simply basks in
the tremendous light and love of the Trinity. In that
Presence we are permeated with the knowledge of God as
Friend and Companion, and of ourselves as sons and
daughters of the Father. It is a listening to the reality of
God *and the self.*


## Listening To Self

What Catherine says next must be understood in the
light of basking in the presence of the Trinity. It is only in
the light of the Trinity that light comes to us; so now *in
that light* we listen to ourselves:

Listen to yourself so as to find the path to God within the
frail walls of your humanity. I don't know how I got the
grace to listen to myself, but I did. It was as if all the
corners of my person were illuminated, and I clearly saw
much in me that wanted to talk to me and that I wanted
to talk to. As the dialogue took place I discovered that it
was really the grace of loving myself!

You cannot really love your neighbor unless you love
yourself first. The Lord said, 'Love your neighbor as
yourself.' In the strange luminosity of the Trinity I
realized that I had to love myself more than I did

because God loved me. I realized too that loving one's self included also loving God who dwells within me. It becomes interwoven, this love affair, like a piece of weaving. The warp and the woof blend in a strange and uncanny way.   (P 157-160)

This "listening to the self" is altogether different from psychological introspection. It is listening to one-self *in the light of the Trinity*. To go into the chambers of the self without faith (which is what a great deal of modern psychiatry and psychology does) can be, and often is, very destructive. To enter your soul without faith in God's presence there, without faith that you are created in God's image, without belief in Christ's power to heal, forgive, etc., can be a very terrifying experience. For Catherine, to listen to the self means discovering that you are lovable — loved by God himself. Strengthened by that truth we can then love ourselves, which is the prelude to loving others properly.

## Listening To Others

There is a sense in which, for Catherine, "hospitality of the heart" is one of the supreme goals of the journey inward. Having been emptied of self and filled with Christ, one is free now to invite into his/her heart all the lonely and wounded of the world in whom the Lord Jesus is present. If we are truly basking in the presence of the Trinity and have come to love ourselves, then we will be able to "listen people into existence."

Listen well, for if you hear his [the Lord's] voice you will be wise with the wisdom of the Lord; and then you will be able to hear the voice of men, not as a surging sea, or as a mob. But each man's speech as his own, a treasure given to you beyond all expectations, because you led yourself to Him and listened to His voice. It is as if God came to prepare you again and again to listen to men. At this moment the Holy Spirit enters with a great strength and vigor. And suddenly the gift of wisdom and discernment becomes like a huge shady tree that grows from your heart, inviting people to sit under it and rest.

With the gift of listening comes the gift of healing, because listening to your brother until he has said the last word in his heart is healing and consoling. Someone has said that it is possible to 'listen a person's soul into existence.' I like that.

These gifts demand an annihilation of the self. One cannot intrude oneself while listening to another. Truly, here the wings of the intellect are folded only to be unfolded by the Holy Spirit who alone knows when this immense gift from God, the intellect, must be used to help the one to whom we are listening. Always the essence of the listener is one of deep reverence, infinite respect, and deep gratitude to God for having selected us for that listening.   (P 159)


Remember that wisdom is love. By listening to God you become a loving person. And then you can allow your love to become a shady tree for others to rest under. This is the first fruits of hospitality: allowing people to rest in your love for them. You may or may not be inspired by the Spirit to "use your intellect" to say something, help them to solve a problem or whatever. The essence of your listening presence is an infinite reverence, love and respect for the other. In our day and age this alone can heal many, since reverence for the individual is one of the missing elements in mass society. "Listening to myself, listening to God, listening to men — all blended into one word — love."

## The Consoler

"He comes to console us. Who is there amongst us who does not need his consolation?"   (SL #74, 1962)

If we have been made for union with God, then loneliness may be the deepest wound.

There seems to be a correspondence in the modern world between the increasing loss of faith in God and loneliness. Nietzsche said that, now that we have killed God, solitude is unbearable. Precisely so. If there is really No One there when we are alone, then the vacuum must be filled with something — noise, TV, distraction of some kind. (Someone asked me once if I had a radio in my poustinia. I said no, it would be a distraction. He said, "From what?") To be alone with the self and all its terrors, and with No One there to be a Companion — to heal, to love — is unbearable indeed.

And the deepest suffering for the Lord may be his apartness from those he has destined for union with him. Catherine goes to Christ to comfort him in his loneliness.

The word "consolation" comes from two Latin words meaning "with" and "alone." "Consolation" basically means to be with someone in his or her aloneness; and that is how we console them, by being with them in a loving way. Contrariwise, the word "desolation" means without someone, the ultimate in aloneness.

In Jewish theology the Messiah was sometimes referred to as the "consolation of Israel." Remember in

St. Luke's Gospel, Simeon in the temple is waiting for the "consolation of Israel." One of the words for Messiah was Consoler.

Many of the promises of Jesus are about coming to dwell in us — "My Father will love you and we will come to you and make our home in you" — in other words, to take away our loneliness. The Gift of all gifts, therefore, is the Consoler, God himself, come to take up his dwelling within us to save us from our radical aloneness. "This is God's dwelling among men. He shall dwell with them, and they shall be his people, and he shall be their God who is always with them. He shall wipe away every tear from their eyes. There shall be no more death, mourning or *desolation*, crying or pain. The former world has passed away" (Rev. 21).

Although this is a vision of the final time, we are called to mediate this consolation of the Consoler to all those who come to us *now* during our earthly pilgrimage. It is only the love of Love Itself who can give us the awesome strength to be an inn for every wounded pilgrim, a shady tree for every tired wayfarer, a heart hospitable to console all the lonely.

> The Promised One had come . . . he whom Jesus Christ called the 'Advocate.' But in Russian as in other languages the word is 'Paraclete,' 'Consoler.' Well, an advocate pleads before a judge, and, it is hoped, consoles the one for whom he pleads. The Father, the Brother, the Consoler. Just think of that! You who are lonely, don't be lonely. You have a Consoler! (Sob 108)

## The Wind As Source Of Adventure

One of the themes of Catherine's spirituality is that our pilgrimage towards the Trinity is a song of poetry, an exciting and thrilling *adventure*. Our earthly journey is not simply a grueling climb up the hill of Calvary. The Spirit tranforms our ascent into an adventure of a lover seeking the Beloved with a song in the heart.

> The Word of Fire that illuminates and warms, the words of the Wind pick us up . . . and bring us right to the top [of the mountain] lest we hurt our feet or fall down. If we listen, then, all the things that we have discussed up to this moment shall become an adventure, shall be full of life; and strength will be given to us beyond our imagination, provided we are open to the Wind and the Fire.

Part of the human condition is to experience the anguish of incompleteness: we are aware that we are limited, and yet we have an infinite longing within us! And we are never satisfied: whatever truth we know, we know there is more to be known. Whatever we love, we know that we can love more, and be loved more. This anguish is holy. This longing is a sign of our transcendence, a manifestation of the Divine within us. It is the Holy Spirit who keeps propelling us along our unending search and journey. Often we don't want to go!

> But I see you draw a line — so far and no further will you go towards God. And there he is, standing in front of you with his arms open, waiting for you to surrender. But there you stand, before some imaginary line you have made for yourself, and you won't move any further. Why? Who can tell? Who can judge? What to do

then? The answer is the Advocate, the Consoler, the Enlightener, the Gift, the Father of the Poor. He and he alone can move your will. Remember, in the life of the Christian, every day is Pentecost. Every day the Mighty Wind comes, if only we will call upon him. Every day the tongues of Flame descend upon us, if only we realize our need of them and desire them with a great desire.   (SL #102, 1962)

The Holy Spirit is pushing, pushing, pushing.   (SLFF #3, 1970)

But now God has decided to really bring him [the pilgrim] up on the mountain of faith. That requires the wind to get him there, the Wind of the Spirit.   (St 81)

Our pilgrimage is also (and always, for Catherine) a journey into the hearts of others, there to bring them the love of Christ:

Yes, listen. Listen to the Wind. You are not alone. Constantly with you, side by side, is the Dove. See, it's the Dove that makes the wind. It's the Wind of his gifts. With them we can enter the heart of another. With the gifts of love and tenderness and of the compassion of God, of Jesus Christ, we can seal the hearts of another to ours as ours is sealed to God's. And so begins a chain of hearts which are sealed to God and to one another. Now there is sobornost, the unity that must exist.   (St. 73)

## The Holy Spirit And Sobornost

We will not treat here Catherine's profound concept of sobornost, unity; but just to mention here that the Holy Spirit is the source of this immense gift:

The Holy Spirit was consolidating the teachings of the Lord. Here, on this immense holy day of the descent of the Holy Spirit upon the apostles, was the opening of their hearts to the parables, his teachings. . . . the Holy Spirit came on Pentecost to begin that new dimension of unity which alone would enable men to follow the narrow path laid out by Jesus Christ, and to understand what 'sobornost' — gathering — really was.   (So 14-15)

## The Spirit And The Splendor Of The Ordinary

For Catherine, God is found primarily in the ordinary, humble duties of everyday life. This is why the mystery of Nazareth is so central for her. God himself, while he was on earth, lived a very ordinary life. So the Father is present in the ordinary. In our "Way of Life," written by Catherine, she sees the Holy Spirit as the One who reveals the splendor of the ordinary:

'I will send down to you him whom the Father has promised. Stay in the city until you are clothed with power from on high.' Do you realize what happened? He told them of the power with which they were going to be clothed, and with which we are clothed too in the sacrament of Confirmation. This Power was not only given to the Apostles. It was given to us, you and me, and that too deepens our mystery; for we are men and women of glory and power provided that we understand the obvious and the commonplace.   (WL)

This theme leads us organically into the next line of the Mandate. For the love of Christ and the splendor of his Gospel shines most brilliantly when we can love "without compromise" in the ordinary things of every day.

CHAPTER FOUR

# DO LITTLE THINGS EXCEEDINGLY WELL FOR LOVE OF ME

[ * * * ]

EVERY LINE of the Mandate is extremely important; or better, every line of the Mandate has its own importance. In my own opinion the great importance of this present line is that it manifests the *universal nature and application* of Catherine's spirituality. It is a Gospel spirituality for all times and for all vocations. Why? Because all the beauty and spiritual richness of the Mandate is brought to bear on *the ordinary actions of everyday life.* Not only brought to bear on them: our ordinary actions are the normal, most consistent places where we meet Christ, live the Gospel, continue our pilgrimage — in short — *the place* where we live out most of our journey to the lonely Christ, and to the hearts of the poor.

Catherine's spirituality is neither lay nor clerical, monastic nor religious, nor any other category. It is a profound Gospel spirituality which can be adapted to every Christian way of life. Herein lies its specifically universal character. It is in this line of the Mandate that this universality is particularly manifested.

We have just finished, in the previous chapter, our consideration of the work of the Holy Spirit in Catherine's vision. In another, shorter commentary on the Mandate, she says that one of the Spirit's principal inspirations concerns the reality of daily living:

> If we listen [to the Spirit] all things shall become an adventure, shall be full of light; and strength will be given to us beyond our imagination, provided we are open to the Wind and the Fire.

> We do these things constantly *in the reality of daily living . . . the little things* of the Spirit . . . that one farther step, that one true smile that comes from the very depth of your heart and not only from your lips. How about that one little touch when your arm is just about numb with the tiredness of the day, and you suddenly see, in a crowd, a sad person, and your body only wants to sit down and not move; but that inner power of the Spirit makes you get up, and inwardly you put your hand out to somebody and say, 'Good night. Sleep well. I will really pray for you because I know you are sad.' Don't forget: 'Do little things well for love of me.'

> The Mandate is like a misty horizon that suddenly, under the influence of the sun, or the fire of the Spirit, extends in depth ever deeper and deeper and deeper. Each one of the words calls you. When you are laid in the grave . . . you will know the dimension of the road you have traveled. It's much greater than the distance between the earth and moon, in fact, the distance is infinite. (TOLM)

It is no exaggeration to say that, for Catherine, the infinite distance which must be traveled to Christ is precisely in the seemingly small acts of saying good night to someone when you are exhausted and hope the person doesn't start talking(!); of reaching out to someone when you notice he or she needs a word or a bit of encouragement. If one does not realize that these are the immense acts which propel us across infinite space towards God, then that person will have missed the very essence of Catherine's vision.

In a letter to the community in 1960 Catherine begged us to listen, listen, listen: "If only you *heard* him," she says. And what does Christ say?

> He says, 'I do not even ask you to watch one hour with Me in my agony. I simply ask you to get out of bed when the alarm rings. I do not ask you to be smitten on your cheeks, nor spat upon. I just ask — beg — you to take correction . . . humbly for love of Me. I do not ask you to be bound to a post and flagellated with leaded whips. I simply ask you to do every task that is given to you with one-hundred percent concentration, complete recollection and thoughtfulness. I do not ask you to hang naked on my Cross, but I ask you to deepen the spirit of poverty in the use of things and the care of creatures. I was stripped naked. Why can't you strip your soul naked of your self-centered thoughts and begin to look upon the world and all things — pots, cups, dust-cloths, food, clothing, all that you have and live by — with deep reverence? You can do that only if you strip yourself naked of self-centeredness and begin to connect creatures, time, work, walking, sitting, sleeping, all that you do, with Me.'

> Today a sentence was going round and round in my head: 'Lord, when will they understand and implement

the connection between your luminous verities of love
and switching off the lights, taking care of clothing,
realizing what is hidden in all these acts?'   (SL #53)

This "connecting everything with Christ" is, for
Catherine, *first* the lesson we must learn in Nazareth:

Lately, I have been thinking much about our vocation,
and it seems to me that it is Nazareth, the hidden, little
village to which we have to go and live with the Holy
Family to become whole again, and to learn about the
'little things' we always talk about, always say must be
done with great love, perfectly, for the love of God. Yes,
there we would learn about little things, and there we
would learn to implement what we are talking about. It
seems to me that each one of us is going to stay there
until we do, right in Nazareth. That is our true
novitiate. Then, if we have made this first step, and
learned the fundamental essence of our vocation, then,
one day, God will say to you, 'Go to Pakistan, go to
Texas, go to the Yukon. There, show my Face to them.'
You see, the *essence of our vocation* is to connect ordinary
and seemingly boring details with Love who is
God.   (SL #53, 1960)

In the monotonous, the hum-drum and ordinary,
*that* is where the Lover and the beloved meet:

'Practical woman,' they say . . . Little do they know that
the cloak of practicality hides the heart of a lover, one
who loves God and man, steadfast and true, that behind
the curtain of things done well for God's love is the path
of one who just loves and loves God and man! Busy,
busy . . . that too. But somewhere deep, hidden away,
lies in this woman a garden enclosed where she and the
Lover are always one; God dwells there. Allelu!   (JI, II)

I found a passage once in William Johnston's *The Inner Eye of Love*, which expressed as well as anything the heart of this line of the Mandate:

> Mystical experience may at first be delightful and filled with froth and joy; but eventually the call comes to go deeper and (wonder of wonders!) this going deeper in all the great mystical traditions is a *passage to the ordinary*. No longer the first exciting silence of discovery but an almost boring silence of penetration and familiarity, a 'becoming at home'. . . . and I wonder if it does not take yet another *enlightenment of the Spirit* to recognize this seemingly hum-drum experience as a real God-experience, and to be faithful to this time of the fallow ground.

Catherine's mysticism (although she would not call it that) is the long journey, under a profound enlightenment of the Holy Spirit, to the ordinary, there to await the Beloved. For it is precisely the ordinary which is the most purifying and constant experience. If mysticism is meeting Christ, then Catherine's spirituality is the immense journey to the ordinary, there to meet the Beloved. I now wish to expand on the main themes in this present line.

## Little Things

Life, from the microscopic to the macrocosmic, is made up of little things — atoms, cells, infinitesimal particles. If you split one little thing — like an atom! — you blow up the whole city. If one little cell in the body becomes diseased, the whole body can become diseased.

When you are in an airplane looking down on a city
you see thousands of tiny buildings; we call them homes.
This is where individual people live. If every home was
healthy, society would be healthy. In the homes are some
individual people. If all the people in that home were
loving towards one another, the home would be a happy
place.

If you want to play a musical score you must play
each note well. You can't simply bang on the piano with
your elbows! Many examples could be given: Life is
made up of countless small things.

And daily life is made up of countless small acts —
rising, eating, working, walking and sitting, etc. One
small act after another. (When quite exhausted once
Catherine said, "It's just one thing after another!") A
scientist knows he must deal with the infinitesimal; and
the musician knows he must deal with each note.

And the seeker after holiness? Part of our pride is
that we can't be bothered with the small things; we must
get on to the big things — whatever those are! Our
spiritual life is "above" little things: we are preparing for
great things. In our spiritual value system we label some
things important and other things unimportant. Being a
superior is important; being under a superior is unimportant. Prayer is important, but manual work is not so
important. Writing books(!) is important, but cleaning
one's room is not important. (One day someone asked St.
Francis de Sales what she could do for Lent. He said,
"Just close doors quietly!")

By "little things" Catherine does not mean small
actions (for example, sweeping a floor) as contrasted
with something "big" (like giving a talk to thirty
thousand people in a stadium). By "little things"
Catherine means *everything*, because in relation to what

God has done for her, everything is a little thing. One of her favorite lines was that of St. Francis: "Lord, I throw myself at your feet and sing and sing that I give you such a small thing." She comments:

> There before my eyes is a crucifix. To me it is living, breathing, full of wounds, and saying to me, 'I love you, I love you.' When I compare my life with that crucifix, then my whole life is nothing. So, to begin with, I consider that the gift of my whole life from the day that he called me to the day that I am speaking to you, *is a tiny thing in proportion to what he gave me.*

> Now, is that clear, what I call a 'little thing'? I think that we misunderstood each other right here. Understand, that, for me, my whole life is as nothing to give — I wish that I had a thousand lives to give him. Now, if I consider that my life is about as big as a thimble, then what is *in it* is still smaller, isn't it? If I consider that my life, which I throw at God's feet, is such a small thing, then *what is inside* cannot be bigger than the whole, can it?

We may think being persecuted for the faith is a big thing. For Catherine it is small. We may think writing books is a big thing. For Catherine it is small. We may think that being invited to give a lecture and being chauffered around like a big-shot is a big thing. For Catherine it is small. Anything that we can give to Christ is small because of what he has done for us.

> So, for me, life is *all* small things . . . I ask: What can a little person do who tries to love God tremendously? I answer, *everything*, from putting the lights off because of holy poverty, to refraining from changing clothes every five minutes because there is a clothing room, to being indifferent to food, to going where God calls you.

## Big Things

I said above that our pride impels us to jump over small things to get to the big things, Catherine, as we have just seen, uses the imagery differently. Everything in relationship to God is small; so in this sense we can only do small things. But then, our small things achieve (you might say) a *spiritual smallness or bigness*, depending on the quality of our *love*. In this sense she says that "sin is a big thing. Anything connected with sin is a big thing, because it hurts love." Sin is a reaching out to achieve a false importance, a false greatness. So sin is a "big thing."

But positively, the true "bigness" which God desires for us is achieved in the *quality of our love*: "The only big thing about you is your hunger to love — to be and do *for God*."

The great key for Catherine is that *every little thing, that is, everything, is connected with loving her Beloved*. This is *the vision of the whole* which dominates and gives meaning to her whole spiritual world:

> Now here again, let us understand one another, for I do not think that we do. First, remember that I have a personal relationship with Christ. To me he is real, is in this room. Besides my faith I have a vivid imagination! For me *he is real*. So there is a knock at the door. Someone is calling for my nursing services. No matter how tired and exhausted I am, *I know that it is God knocking! I literally see his hand with a wound.*

> Another example. I have empty hands. At night I consider that I have to bring something to the altar for tomorrow's paten. What can I bring? I can bring a thousand buttons well-sorted with great love, understanding full well that because of my attention these

buttons have redemptive value. I can bring hours of conversation with you. I can bring many letters with attention to details. This faith comes from a tremendous personal understanding that God is real and my tremendous Lover. He has first given his life for me. In the face of that gift I am like one who is bereft of my senses! I go around gathering every flower so that I can bring it to him. It never occurs to me that you can possibly separate anything from love.   (SL #104, 1962)

By its very Mandate given to me, Madonna House is dedicated to the restoration of the whole world to Christ by doing little things with great love for God and man. It is not what you do that matters; it is what you are. If you have understood the romance and the immensity of little things, you will restore the world to Christ. By being a light, adventuresome, joyous, glad, simple, humble, taking on the little things; they become big because they are done for God.   (SL #177)


Love is the heart of the Gospel; and the word "love" occurs four times right at the heart of the Mandate. Catherine's teaching about doing everything with great love is not new. But she expands upon our tradition and places purity of heart at the center of her incarnational spirituality.

It is not new. The Lord said, "Well done, good and faithful servant, you have been faithful in small matters, I will set you over many. Enter into the joy of your Master." St. Paul has that magnificent hymn to love where he says (as beautifully as it is possible to say), that whatever is not done with love is nothing.

One of my favorite sayings from our tradition is from Pascal, because it brings out the fact that Christ is acting in us, and it is this Presence which gives the proper spiritual outlook on our actions: "To do the small things as though they were great, on account of the majesty of Jesus Christ who does them in us and who lives our life; and the great things as though they were small and easy, on account of his omnipotence." Jesus acting in us, and we acting out of love for him! What immense dignity our actions have!

In our own time, the Little Flower, St. Therese of the Child Jesus, is one of the greatest pilgrims who traveled through the infinite spaces to the ordinary. What a marvel of grace! She achieved what all the spiritual masters say is the heart of everything: to will only one thing: pure love.

## "The Vision Of The Whole"

This is Catherine's symbol for a whole cluster of spiritual truths which, rightly understood, do indeed form the "very essence of the apostolate," as she has often said. It is a spiritual awareness, first, that everything we do has a redemptive value; and, secondly, that doing every little thing well is a preparation for our call to help in the healing and the restoration of the human heart.

Once Catherine came across a pile of material that the community had been reckless and negligent in caring for. She wrote:

A mantle of fear and trembling fell upon my soul. It seemed to me that I was lying prostrate before the Lord and that, with a sad and severe countenance, he was saying to me: 'Behold, you have failed to teach them two things: the relationship between such thoughtlessness and sanctity, and the relationship between tidiness and penance which restores my world to me.'

How in heaven's name can an apostle of Madonna House develop the sixth sense, that empathy and sympathy so necessary in dealing with the untidiness of a thousand wounds in human souls, if they cannot take care of coats, shoes, and miscellaneous articles that they leave around so easily? How can they heal the whole person — a work to which they have dedicated their lives — if they do not realize the connection between untidiness and poverty? Their life is that of restoring order to the world for Christ.

When you serve at table . . . do it quietly and efficiently. If you learn to serve that way, and connect serving to the supernatural order, you will grow greatly in wisdom and love, and you will be a light shining in the darkness of the world. The light of your loving service will lead people to God.

My parents never let us forget that every task, however ordinary, was of redeeming, supernatural value, if done out of love. But why should I give you my poor, sinful self as an example when you are surrounded by marvelous books about the glorious saints of God? Many were canonized by the Church because they had the 'vision of the whole,' that is, they perfectly and constantly acted out of love.

You see, this is the essence of our vocation . . . to connect an ordinary and seemingly boring life (with its repetitious details) with Love Who is God. Then a day at the typewriter, when your back is aching and your mind reeling with tiredness, is a day that has redeemed many souls; how many, God alone knows. We must have that awareness and make that connection.

Tell me, how are you going to restore the world to Christ — the tremendous world of souls — if you have to be told daily (if not hourly) that the boxes in the left-hand corner of the hallway should be taken every morning to a certain place? How are you going to restore the world to Christ if your workshops or the clothing room, or the dishes or the kitchen, reflect the disorder of your souls? How can you be aware of the world of souls if you are not aware of the fact that, when it snows, it would be a good idea to shovel a path and clear the steps? How are you going to restore the world to Christ if you are doing the minimum required — the letter of the law — and never plunge into its spirit? In a word, Christ is waiting for you to become aware of him and of the apostolate that he has confided to you by becoming aware of the connection between brooms, dishwasher, letter-typing, tidiness — and the restoration of the world. (SL #53, 1960)

Our vocation is to do little things well for the love of God. This means monotonous things eternally repeated. But if we have the 'vision of the whole' we will connect doing these little things, these monotonous things, with spiritual truths. The vision of the whole is that every task, routine or not, is of redeeming value, supernatural value, because we are united with Christ. But we must *stay aware* of this truth. (PTW, 18)

## The Romance Of The Ordinary

At the beginning of our pilgrimages we are not spiritually mature enough to see our Beloved in the ordinary. We dreams of great things, that is to say, we have illusions:

You dream of great deeds. Everyone, for example, reads about Charles de Foucauld. Many have a starry-eyed look. They wonder if they shouldn't become a Little Sister or Brother of Charles de Foucauld. But when I listen to their conversations I want to cry. Not one of them stops to think of what a heroic life he really led. He lived in a little hut in the blistering desert, with its cold and sering nights, amongst strange, primitive human beings. All this means hanging on a cross for years instead of hours; but nobody seems to be aware of this. Most just see the romance of his life, not the reality.  (SL #53, 1960)

What Catherine seeks to teach people — challenge people to seek — is to find the thrill of being with the Beloved in the ordinariness of every day:

I will speak of cups, because you seem to have an aversion to washing dishes. If you have the attitude that this is a beautiful little thing that you can give to God, then washing a cup becomes an adventure. It is this sense of adventure, glory and joy that you lack.

I have lots of fun. I might be terribly tired, and the job might be monotonous, but I will make it interesting for myself. For example, many of you saw the terrible monotony of the library work down in the basement before Christmas. You saw that I was sometimes tense, and sometimes, perhaps, a bit sharp, for which I was sorry. Nevertheless, I kept thinking to myself, 'Gee, this is wonderful! Generations of our members are going to benefit from this.' Again, a little thing to give to God.

Now, do you get the picture, or are you still missing the point of what I mean by 'little things'? The whole of life is a 'little thing' which we throw at God's feet and sing and sing. Every little thing should be done perfectly, completely connected with God, for otherwise it ceases to be interesting. It has no sense and no being.

There is great freedom in this. You don't have to 'smile' doing the little things. The very fact that, in your hearts you enjoy doing them, will radiate in your eyes, will show forth in your concentration.   (SL #76, 1962)

An interesting thought by Catherine: If we do not act out of love our actions have "no sense and no being." It is love for the Beloved that gives *being* to our actions. "It all hinges on God as Person, on the sense of adventure, the sense of call. . . ."   (*Ibid.*)

## Little Things As Gifts And Music For The Christ Child

This is one of the best examples I have found which reveals how Catherine is able, by faith and love, to see the magnificence of the ordinary, see it for what it truly is — a gift and a song for the Beloved.

The strange path of monotonous little duties of everyday that could become, if we made them so, gifts more precious even than the three Kings brought him: dishwashing, filing, running around from one meeting to another, answering bells, dealing with people all day long. Yet, all these things could become a cascade of gems precious beyond men's reckoning, of gold too heavy for man's hands to carry, of grains of incense that would cover the earth *if only our hearts touched his heart, and opened themselves wide to being loved by him and loving him back.*

You see, I think of you as minstrels, learning to sing
lullabies to the Christ Child. The notes of your songs are
your daily work, and the attitudes that you bring to it.
And I pray that no sour notes ever come to your songs to
the Christ Child.

I see you as cherished by his Mother who waits for you to
come and share not only her Christmas joy in the stable
of Bethlehem but her whole life, so hidden and immense. For it is she who has called us to pattern our lives
on that of herself, her Son, and Joseph — in Nazareth —
as a humble life, a hidden life, *life composed of daily,
ordinary little things, but oh! how well done! and with what
great love!*

I see you as musical instruments perfectly attuned to the
will of God. Instruments that make a concert, make
beautiful music in this strange, silent world of ours. I
think of you as beautiful notes in the beautiful melody
of the Holy Spirit.    (SL #51, 1959)

In a letter in 1946 to her then spiritual director, Fr.
Paul Furfey, Catherine gives another marvelous example of how she puts the delicacy of love and beauty into
doing little things well: "The older I get the more clearly
I see the importance of little things. Often when I look at
my Lady Charity these days I see that her garments are
composed of so many tiny pieces that only love could
have woven into the shimmering dress she wears."    (FL,
1946)    Each one of us, depending on our own relationship with the Lord, depending on our sense of love-
making, will be inspired by the Spirit how to make each
one of our actions a concrete act of love.

In *The Way of Divine Love* there is an event in the life
of Josefa Menendez which perfectly fits in here. She was
going about doing her tasks when Our Lord appeared to

her and asked her what she was doing. She said she was closing the windows. He said: "Wrong answer, Josefa. You are coming from love and going to love." That particular corridor is known to this day as the corridor of love. And so it should be with all our actions.

I would say that this passage to the ordinary, this immense pilgrimage to the Beloved present in every action, is at the very heart of Catherine's *asceticism*. She believes, of course, in fasting and prayer and all the other practices of the spiritual life. But what are they all *for*? They are "all for" awareness of the Beloved at every moment and in every circumstance. (Because of the extreme importance of this line I have included, in the Appendix, Catherine's best statement on this aspect of the Mandate.)

## The Painful Refinery Of Love

Anyone who has ever tried, in the slightest, to purify his or her ordinary actions, and act only out of love for Jesus, knows how demanding such a road is.

> Well do I know, dearly beloved, the intense discipline, mortification and penance that such minute and boring tasks entail: sorting buttons, separating safety pins from straight pins, sorting in the clothing room, and working in the library over small and painstaking details. Yes, for thirty years I have learned the immense and ineffable lessons of love in the school of infinitely small details.   (SL #53, 1960)

Catherine says that if we don't learn how to love here in the nitty-gritty of every day, "we may not go to hell, but we will go into the painful refinery of love — to the terrible school of love — purgatory. We must learn love either here or there. Not to learn it at all is hell" (SL #53, 1960). Although Catherine calls *purgatory* the "refinery of love," I think the phrase is well suited also to the furnace, the forge, of trying to love completely in our ordinary actions. We have our choice of one of two purgatories: either this "terrible school of love," this "refinery of love," here and now, or the one hereafter.

There is also the cross. I should speak about that also. I cannot visualize a love story with God without a cross. To me the cross is *the thing!* I desire it, I accept it, and I ask for the grace never to fear it, because one day I shall know its joy. God embraced the cross because he wanted to. For this he was born! For this we are born — to lie on it with him. I literally mean the words that I say, but I don't think you understand me. That's why you have a problem with 'little things.'

When somebody says to me, 'Catherine, I don't think that I can take a lifetime of these little things. It's excruciating,' I want to weep. It's a failure to understand our *faith*. The same person, whoever he or she is, will have a lifetime of other little things [wherever he or she goes] that will be just as excruciating. However, never think of your vocation as a lot of monotonous 'little things.' Think of it as the glory of the cross. Measure the 'little things' against his bigness — *what he has done for us.* Try every minute to put a little grain of sand before the altar. Before you die you might have a mountain to offer. It's so simple! (SL #104, 1962)

## The "Duty Of The Moment"

The "duty of the moment" is Catherine's symbolic phrase for each moment seen from the perspective of the Father's will: We can only, completely and entirely, offer each moment to the Beloved if we are doing what the Beloved wants us to do.

> Surrender means doing the will of the Beloved. Using that inner hearing, that inner ingenuity of love, that intuition of love to almost anticipate the will of the Beloved. Because the will of the Beloved is . . . the perfection of our vocation to love in Madonna House. It is expressed in a passionate desire that flames inside like an unquenchable fire . . . *to live perfectly the duty of every moment of our state in life.*

> You may say at this point, 'Here she goes again, talking about little things.' Yes, you are right! But by now you should know that the little things I talk about are immense. And they are immense because they deal with God and the things of God; they deal with the love of God and our love for him. What could be greater, bigger, more immense than that!

> Let's face it! In the natural order we might have moments of excitement in Madonna House or in one of our foundations; but by and large there is a sameness to our life. The repetitiousness of our daily tasks would not hold our attention, nor our interest, especially since there is no tangible remuneration of any kind attached to them in the natural order.

> How then can we utterly surrender? We must strip ourselves. How? We must become contemplatives. The word 'contemplative' simply means thinking about something of importance to us, someone we cherish,

someone dear. Whatever it is, it means being absorbed in this particular person or this particular situation. (SL #116, 1962)

Here Catherine identifies the *awareness* she has been speaking about, with *prayer*. (We will be discussing prayer in the last few lines of the Mandate.) Suffice to point out here that the doing of little things well, meeting the Beloved in the duty of the moment, means a deepening of one's prayer. "Poustinia of the heart" is her prayer — symbol for doing the duty of the moment in contemplative awareness of the Beloved.

## The Duty Of The Moment As Our Strategic Place

"Strategy" is a word often used in connection with warfare. We are in a spiritual combat. Catherine uses the word sometimes when, for seemingly good motives, we are tempted to disregard God's present will and get involved in things he is not asking. "Satan tempts people by good when he cannot tempt them to evil."

. . . The duty of the moment is our strategic place. Perhaps no strategy will avail us, but still, there remains this one thing — that God has given into our hands *today*. God has given us today, and today we must do the duty of the moment . . . just one day at a time. It is *in this day* that we have to love God as God love us. *This is the day* when we have to open our hearts like doors and take everyone in that we can.    (MHWWI, 30)

To clarify this. There were several occasions when tragedies happened, in this case, the Cuban missile crisis.

People got nervous and upset. What are we to do in the face of such news? The duty of the moment.

> Those of us who are removed from the seat of the con-
> flict [the missile crisis] at a given moment must then go
> about their business, which is the business of God, as
> they have done in the days of peace. For the greatest
> contribution that we can make at that moment is to go
> about the duty of the moment, which is the duty of God,
> and offer it up for the same intentions as our
> prayers.   (SL #130, 1963).

Another occasion was the assassination of Robert Kennedy:

> I was in a sort of state of shock. I wanted to ask Fr. Cal's
> permission to sleep it off, to try to forget the horror of it
> all — but it wasn't the will of my Father. The will of my
> Father was that I offer the day . . . according to the duty
> of the moment. And the duty of the moment that day
> was to begin sorting. . . . It is of such things that I want
> you to think in depth. We must fully understand that
> the simple, little things, the duty of the moment in your
> house and in Madonna House, *is the answer for that atone-
> ment* [that is, for the shooting of Kennedy].   (SL #250,
> 1968)

Or, to take another example. One of the younger women in one of our houses was concerned about all the poor women she saw in town and thought she should do something for them. (The house was already involved in helping them in different ways, but this person was troubled that Madonna House was not doing enough.)

I tried with my life and with my words to preach one thing and preach it loudly, clearly; but I guess it wasn't very clear, and I wasn't loud enough. . . . However, I will repeat it once more: Madonna House is the place of little things done well for the love of God, etc., etc., etc. In order to create the Community of Love — the Christian community of love that is our aim — *we must always do the will of our Father like Christ did! It is through total concentration on the daily duty of the moment, on the will of the Father, which puts us in truth, and therefore in Christ. That is how we can help those women. This is the mystery of love.* (*Ibid.*)

When our desires to help people are bigger then our capacities, we can best help them by doing the duty of the moment, the will of the Father. Offering this in union with Christ — to whom we are joined by doing the Father's will — is the very best thing we can do for them. Again, as the life of the Little Flower shows, it is the quality of love which radiates out into the spiritual world. Doing little things well is the immense journey into purity of heart in the ordinary.

CHAPTER FIVE

# LOVE — LOVE — LOVE

[ * * * ]

I CHOSE this line of the Mandate as the title for the present book because, as we have already seen, love is the central message of the Gospel and daily life. The Gospel is about the Father's tremendous love for us revealed in Jesus Christ; about the Spirit, who is the very Love between the Father and the Son, and who opens the Gospel words to our understanding, and by his love impels us along the road of our pilgrimage. Then, in the fourth line, we saw that the heart of Catherine's asceticism is *loving* in each and every moment of life. This present line — Love, Love, Love — is Catherine's way of emphasizing, beyond any misunderstanding, that *love is the very heart of the Gospel.*

Catherine has said that the first line of the Mandate is the major theme; the other lines are commentaries on the first line. Thus, there are seven lines of commentary — and this line about love is at the very center of those lines. In this present line love is not so much defined as

*emphasized*. The whole rest of the Mandate is a description of the various forms which love takes.

Pilgrimaging, poverty, identification with the poor,
littleness, simplicity, listening to the Spirit, doing little
things well — what are these except ways of loving? Since
love is the name we give to that ultimate movement
towards union; the name we give to that union itself —
being "in love"; the name we give even to God himself,
"for God is love," we can say that every kind of striving
towards God is love. We give the virtues different names
to emphasize different aspects of our loving.

The infinite Ocean of Life from which we have all
come is Love Itself. Our faith is that, to each one of us at a
given moment, Love said: "Come forth." Love is the
origin of our being. I don't know anything about genetic
engineering, or about computer programming. But
maybe we could put it this way: We have all been pro-
grammed to love; every part of our genetic code is
stamped with love; and the deepest movement of every
cell within us tends towards love. The very last line of
Dante's magnificent poem, the Divine Comedy, speaks
about the "love which moves the planets and the stars."

When the Lord Jesus was asked about the greatest
commandment of the law, he stated the basic code of all
being. As we know, he put it in a commandment form —
"Love the Lord your God. . . ." But could we not also say
his reply means this: "All conscious being tends towards
God with all its heart, with all its mind, with all its soul,
with all it strength. All conscious being tends towards
love of other conscious beings as towards oneself." As
well as a command, was he not also stating the inner law
of our being, written into the very fiber of every cell?

"As the Father has loved me, so I have loved you.
Remain in my love." It is all about loving.

The Vatican Council II Decree on the Religious Life concerning those who live according to the three evangelical counsels, defines their way of life (in the very first words) as those engaged in the "pursuit of perfect love." Catherine would have approved that definition very much for the goal of her own spiritual children.

The word "love" occurs three times in this line. My own opinion is that this is for *emphasis — love is the most important reality.*

In years of meditation on the Mandate, members of our community have applied the three loves to the Persons of the Trinity, to our three promises of poverty, chastity, and obedience, and to love of God, neighbor, and self. The Holy Spirit delights to speak intimately to each of us at given times; but in Catherine's writings I do not find any specific application of the three loves. What we do find is her emphasizing that *love is everything.*

## The Apostolate Is Love

The following is from our "Way of Life," the principal document Catherine has left us concerning the nature of our apostolate:

Love is the very essence of being brought together by the Lord. In my estimation the primary work of the Apostolate is that we love one another. For this reason we are pilgrims in the world. For this reason we travel in poverty. For this reason we find security only in Christ. It's for this reason we journey in chastity to serve and love Christ in others. It's for this reason we live in obedience, to serve only the will of God. That is the greatest work of the Apostolate. We must love God and love ourselves according to the will of God; and we must love one another. Then we shall be icons of Christ. People will want from us just the sight of our loving God, ourselves and one another. It is not our Constitution that attracts people; it is our love, our trying to love God as he wants us to love him. And let's make sure that we understand what we're talking about. 'Why do you want to put in the Constitution what's so obvious?' you may ask. 'Everybody knows that we have to love God.' Yes, everybody *knows*; but show me what everybody *does*. Our primary work is love.   (WL)

There is only one way that I shall restore the world. The key is this intangible reality — which is as strong as death, as strong as everlasting life — and it is called *love*. Nothing can destroy it, unless we destroy it ourselves. It is the only motive, the only reason, for being here. Everything else is senseless unless you are here for loving — utterly, passionately, completely. . . .

If people ask you 'What is the Apostolate of Madonna House?' the answer is simple: It is an apostolate to love. And where love is, God is. And we desire to be God in the midst of the world. We are dedicated to the restoration of the world — man and his institutions — to God. The only way we can restore them is by loving, by having God within ourselves, a living flame. The rest will follow. That's all there is to it.   (SL #140, 1956)

In the early stages of our journey towards God we give the movements of the heart various names — virtues, we call them. As we journey, everything blends into one movement — love. The following is from a letter Catherine wrote to her then spiritual director, Fr. Paul Furfey:

I asked St. Mary Magdalene to show me how to follow in
her footsteps . . . so that of me also the only memory
would be that I loved much and well. . . . The older I get,
the more my heart hungers just for Caritas. All other
things seem to have fallen somewhere by the side of the
road, that long, long road of life that has been mine. But
Charity is still my one love, my great goal. For her sake I
must go on, I cannot stop. For my heart is in love now
more than ever with Love, and, of course, that means
God.   (FL, 1946)

Love is a strange fire, it burns, now vividly, now
flamboyantly, now banking fire and light. Love walks all
roads, and it stands at all crossroads. The walking and
the standing are part of loving. For everywhere men
seek it at all times. Love does not die. It is again on fire
and ready to light their path. They do not know its heat
and warmth is this endless holocaust.   (JI, II)

In a recent magazine interview with the three people
principally responsible for our community at this time,
the question was asked: " 'What is the fundamental
charism of the community?' Albert Osterberger: Love.
Father Robert Pelton: Love. Jean Fox: Love." (CCR,
301)   Catherine would have been most pleased with the
answer!

"And above all let us enter the school of Bethlehem
and Nazareth, to grow in the one thing that matters —
LOVE. For, after all, life is but a dialogue of LOVE . . .
between God and us . . . an encounter of LOVE." (SL
#34, 1958)

On this lovely day [Holy Thursday] let us try to understand the immense joy of our humble, hidden vocation

> . . . let us begin to realize that it is indeed a vocation to
> love, first love one another, and then all men. He ad-
> dresses the words of the Last Supper to us — asking us to
> love one another in the loveless marketplace so that
> men in the heat of the day and the cold of the night . . .
> could see his love for us and ours for him and one
> another and warm themselves at it. . . . That is our
> humble, simple, glorious, joyous vocation.  (SL #73,
> 1961)

"This is love: not that we loved God, but that he
loved us" (1 Jn 4:10).

I mentioned above that to "preach the Gospel without compromise" also means for Catherine to preach the
*Gospel* and not your own ideas. What strikes one in all her
teaching is this *Gospel authenticity.* I think nowhere is this
more evident than in her comprehensive teaching about
love. It is the cliche of all cliches today to say that the
word "love" has been abused. Catherine did *not* abuse it!
She saw, with the eyes of Christ, what love was.

It is not possible to completely separate themes in
Catherine's writings. One aspect of her religious genius
was to see, live, and teach the interpenetration of all
themes. We probably all experience them that way, as a
complex whole; but the Western mind (in particular)
thinks it necessary to speak about this complexity in some
kind of ordered way! Catherine's mind was different. So,
some of the things I will quote now have already been
slightly touched upon in the previous sections (especially
the section on the Gospel). What I wish to do now is give a
sort of comprehensive picture of the dominant ways
Catherine spoke about love.

## God Is Love

Love originates in God. Love is not first and foremost what we have done or are doing. Love first of all is what God has done for us: "This is the love I mean: not our love for God, but God's love for us when he sent his Son to be the sacrifice that takes away our sins." God's overwhelming love for us dominated Catherine's whole life and spiritual journey:

> Yet, I cannot stop, for I must proclaim *the Good News*, that God loved us first . . . that he emptied himself for us out of love . . . to save us and redeem us . . . to bring us to a life of union with him here and hereafter. Nor can I ever stop repeating that we must love him back . . . that we must empty ourselves . . . that we must allow him to fill us so that we might show him to others, so that they too may love him and be united with him. THIS IS THE ESSENCE OF OUR APOSTOLATE. THIS IS OUR GOAL. THIS IS THE SPIRIT OF MADONNA HOUSE! (SL #74, 1961)

For the believer, for the Christian, life is a relationship to God, a response to God. Nothing — no concept, no creature, not the self — nothing can be understood properly without its reference to God. It is the same with love. Until we know that God exists, that he is Love, that he loves us, that he has sent his Son into the world to be our Savior — until we know, in some kind of living way *these truths, we do not really know what love is.* You may be able to write beautiful poetry about love, describe sublime inner experiences of love. But until one knows with a living knowledge that God is Love and has sent Love into the world to die for us all, one does not know the deepest reality or nature of love.

I think one of the modern heresies (practical if not theoretical) is a belief, an attitude, that one cannot have a *direct* relationship with God himself. All relations now must pass through other people. One truth (among others) which the Holy Spirit is helping to restore through movements such as the charismatic renewal concerns this transcendent nature of our relationship with God. In Eastern Orthodox Christianity, this transcendent relationship with God is very much emphasized.

For all Catherine's emphasis on loving Christ in the other, she never succumbed to the *reduction* of one's relationship to God with the relationship with the other. God is God. Christ is Christ. The neighbor is the neighbor. Christ is *in* the neighbor, but he is not absorbed *by* the neighbor. In her poetry, in her prayer life, Catherine has a powerful, direct, personal love relationship with *God himself.* It is her experience of this *direct, transcendent* love which is the dynamism behind her life.

> I love you, Christ of mystery and flame. I love you utterly. Utterly surrendered, I rest at peace in mystery and fire, knowing only that this is my place. I love you, Christ, desired one of nations, whose prefigurations began with the dawn of time. I love you, Christ of mystery and flame. Bridegroom of souls, in your arms I rest, a soul in love. O great Love, how can such a small thing as I find a nestling place within your embrace? I love you, Christ of mystery and flame. I love you with a passion that spills in torrents from my soul and changes into a white flame of pain when I behold you crucified, bleeding for the sins of all. I love you, Christ of mystery and flame, my Lord and God, with my whole being. I have forgotten all the past. The future? What is that? I

love but for this moment, this instant, when, reposing
on your heart, I hear your heartbeats telling me you
love me too, while I can go and do the 'duty of the
instant, of the moment,' for you.   (L 16-17)

When Jesus was asked about the great commandment, most of what he said was about loving *God*. Every
other love must be ordered by, seen in the light of,
dominated by, our love for God. Without this proper,
transcendent ordering we will not love our neighbor
aright, will not have the power to love in the truth.

Domus Dominae — the House of Our Lady — is a house
of love. . . . All those who dwell in it are lovers of Christ,
her divine Son. All have but one goal, one thought, one
flaming desire — TO LOVE GOD MADLY. For everyone
realizes that there is so little time on earth to do so.   (SL
#11, 1957)

## Love One Another

Loving the people with whom we live is the hardest
task of all. (A friend of mine recently visited a Carmelite
convent and spoke with a Sister in her 90's, one of the
original members of the community. She said: "Do you
know what is the hardest thing of all? The Sisters!")
It is commonly said that it is hard to live with a saint.
Actually, from our experience, we know it is hard to live
with anybody! With unerring and relentless Gospel wisdom Catherine has always insisted that, after our love for
God, love for one another is the first work of the Apostolate and the Gospel.

Our Lord sent his apostles out two by two so that they could learn to love one another first. For it would be utterly useless for them to try to 'love the world' and 'bring it the glad tidings of love, of the Gospel,' if they did not first apply that Gospel of love to themselves and loved one another as God wants us to love one another — totally, without holds barred.   (SL #63, 1960)

I remind you once more, Dearly Beloved Children of my Spirit, that each foundation is only as strong as the love and trust and openness and obedience and joy that reigns among you, and that is given to your director. If that openness, that trust, that love are not here — no matter how great the activity — that house will not grow inwardly in wisdom and in grace before God.

For we do not evaluate the 'success' of a foundation by its physical growth; that should be the fruit of inward growth. Unless this latter is present, the first will be very shallow. The foundation is growth in love. . . .

We must feed, give drink, clothe, visit *each other* in a given house — with a great, immense, flaming love. If we don't, then the house is empty, like sounding brass and tinkling cymbals. But even emptier than the house are our hearts, souls, and minds. We are a living lie, apostles who do not love one another . . . who profess before the world that they are lovers of Christ, whereas in truth they walk alone in the dark night of their own making, without the light of caritas, which, we must always remember, is a Person — God himself.   (SL #92, 1962)

Today [Holy Thursday] is Love's day. Today God has shown us *how much he loves us!* Shown it by dying on the Cross. Showing us how we must love him and one another! Try to remember how many times Christ repeated the word love. *How many times he asked us to love one another as he and the Father love one another?* How many times did he repeat it, so gently yet so strongly: A new commandment I give you, that you love one another.

There is only one yardstick of sanctity in our apostolate — how much do we love God, and how much do we first love one another, and then others? For we cannot love the poor and not love one another.   (SL #18, 1957)

## ... And Love Your Neighbor

After reminding us that the people we live with are our first neighbors, Catherine emphasizes, as does the Lord in the Gospel, that everyone we pass on the road of life is our neighbor. The following passage combines many themes, and will serve as a good brief summary of her teaching here:

Man is on a pilgrimage, seeking others like himself with the same needs. Actually, the need of man today is the need to be loved. We pass by, without even noticing one another. Without stopping. Without the slightest sign of recognition. That is why man comes daily closer to despair, and why he frantically continues to search for the one who will love him.

The search is for God. But God isn't easily found if he isn't reflected in the eyes of men. It is time that Christians began to take notice of everyone they meet. For each person is his sister and brother in Christ. Each person must be 'recognized.' Each person must be given a token of love and friendship, be it just a smile, a nod of the head, or the total availability that Christians must offer to their brothers and sisters if they are to fulfill the hunger of men for God. Christians must be 'icons of Christ.'

But love must be given with deep reverence, irrespective of the status of the person encountered. Reverence, understanding, the hospitality of one's heart — these are the immediate, intense needs of men today.   (R, Sept., 1971)

Man is capable of a universal love. The men and women called to this universal love open their hearts to the other, completely. Who is the other for them? Their neighbor. Who is their neighbor? The world, composed of all the individuals who need them. This universal love begins with falling in love with Christ, and then, for his sake, loving all people in the person of one's neighbor. The neighbor is whoever comes to the door.   (SL #154, 1964)

I said in the first chapter that to preach the Gospel means to make Christ present. In our relationships with our neighbor, Christ is made present through love. Through the journey inward, through the discipline of Nazareth and all the other purifications of our life with God, we are emptied of the false self and filled with Christ. We become "icons of Christ." By loving others, the love of Christ is made present to them.

How can I love if there is one millionth of an ounce of self in me? For love, you know, is a Person. Love is God. Where love is, God is. And so our vocation is to make room for God in our self. If I may say so — clothe God with our flesh. To give him hands and lips and eyes

again, and a voice. But to do that we must die to self. For
God is immense. He needs much room! Our whole being! And so, there is our vocation. To burn, to die, so as
to become a flame, so as to make room for Christ to grow
in us.  (SL #140, 1956)

This section on what is so fundamental and so all-
pervasive in Catherine's spirituality — love of neighbor
— will be brief. Because, actually, the whole Mandate is
an intricate, wonderful doctrine on how the love of God
and love of neighbor continually feed, influence and
interpenetrate one another. There is hardly any moment
in her thinking about God when the neighbor is far away.
I will give just two of many possible examples. And I give
them, not so much for the content as to show that, for
Catherine, love of God and love of neighbor are intimately intertwined. Love of neighbor is not one of the
virtues for Catherine: it is an *essential ingredient* of love
for God.

Thus, when she is alone:

Charity does not depend on my seeing you. I love you
across time and space. We think that charity is physical
contact. It is that. But charity doesn't need contact. In
the night, when I can't sleep, I smell the dust of India
and the taste of cold rice is on my tongue. I hear the
modern weapons whistle over Vietnam as I heard them
in the last War. I am that woman who is hiding under a
tree with a child, and I see my house blown up. I am in
South Africa suffering from apartheid. When I love
there is no space, no place where I cannot go, where I
am not the other.   (Private Talk, August, 1965)

Even her loneliness is a grace — reminding her of the loneliness of Christ, of others, and impelling her towards assuaging the thirst of others for God:

> The land of loneliness is the land of joy. The land of loneliness is the land of union with God. The land of loneliness is the land of hunger for God. The land of loneliness is the land of belonging to God and understanding that God alone matters. The land of loneliness is a fantastic place that words cannot describe. Really but at the same time it is the land of belonging to God.

> I think the secret of that land is that the hunger for God grows like a fire — is a fire. At the same time the love for humanity intensifies, and there is only one thought in the land of loneliness — to lead men to God. And I think that's why it's called the 'land of loneliness.'

> In the land of loneliness there is only one thought, one goal, one dream that matters, and that is *leading people to God*. It's a passion. It's the only desire; but people do not go to God. And that's why it's the land of loneliness. I think this is the loneliness that Christ experienced before his death, and probably during his whole life; certainly in Gethsemane.

> To know a little bit about who God is is to *passionately desire to give him to all of humanity*. It is to try to give him to the best of one's ability, but then discover that men do not want to accept him totally. They only want to give God a small token of themselves.

> And so one walks in the land of loneliness. To desire to lead men to God — that is the land of loneliness. (Unpublished Talk, 1971)

There are so many reasons why Catherine's spirituality is the Spirit's inspiration precisely *for our times*. One

of them is the contemporary experience of loneliness. It
may well be true (for the westernized cultures at least)
that never before has loneliness been such a burning,
devastating experience. Lack of faith, mass society, im-
personalism, the breakup of families, constant moving,
shunting the elderly, the sick, the marginal into institutions and ghettoes, secular psychoanalysis (going into
the self without faith, without God) — and many other
factors — all contribute to an isolation, a loneliness of the
human person on a massive scale, and to a depth perhaps
new in the history of our Western civilization. Loneliness
is now one of the diseases of the modern world.

Catherine's own experience of loneliness — and it
was intense — becomes a grace. It identifies her with the
loneliness of Christ who weeps because men do not come
to God in their need. But this experience of the loneliness of Christ impels Catherine to even greater efforts to
reach others in their isolation. She is constantly and
simultaneously desiring both God and the salvation of
others.

The common theme of the above quotations is expressed in Catherine's phrase — "the hospitality of the
heart" — and this symbolic phrase comes very close to
the center of her teaching.

In the third volume of this series I hope to show how,
for Catherine, in *this life*, the lonely Christ *in the other* is
the ever-recurring center to which her love returns. The
journey inward is finally revealed as the journey into the
"marketplace," which, as she will say, is the human heart.
The second last line of the Mandate says, "Go . . . into the
depths of men's hearts. . . ." This is where the love
of Christ needs to be experienced and "preached" most
of all — in the depths of human hearts. The Mandate
has everything to do with how to make this enormous,

perilous, and almost infinite journey into the land of
loneliness of the human heart:

> Love, the mother of all virtues. Love the fire that alone
> can push back the darkness of the powers and
> principalities. Who shall venture into the kingdom of
> death and hate . . . real death . . . death to the soul? Only
> the one who would die to self because he loves; and
> hence, obedient to the will of God he becomes a light, a
> torch, a bonfire, unafraid to walk alone into the dark-
> ness and conquer hate! *There is only one thing that con-
> quers hate and that's love. Nothing else ever will.*

## Compassion

There are several dimensions of loving which
Catherine writes about that, if I had space, would fit in
very well here. *Tenderness, mercy, gentleness with others* are
very close to the essence of love. There is one dimension,
however, that is closer than all of these, one aspect of love
which leads us naturally into the phrase, "not counting
the cost." It is the beautiful love-dimension of *compassion*.

You will recall that it's the *passionate love of Christ*
which transforms the Christian life into a wonderful
adventure:

> Passion makes love sparkle and shine, leading it to the
> rugged tops of immense mountains that lie in the hearts
> of men but can only be scaled by passionate lovers.
> [Note: the journey is into the hearts of others.] Its roots
> are love, its fruit is love. Christ loved us *passionately*, and
> some of us love him back passionately.

Passion usually means pain. Nothing strange about that. Love and passion not only hold hands, not only scale the tops of rugged mountains, but they are entwined one around the other. There is no love without pain, and no pain without love. One without the other is inconceivable: love without pain is inconceivable. (P 170)

Then she presents Mary to us as our model of compassion:

Mary enters into this marriage of love and passion which the Lord accepted and through which he redeemed us. Pure of heart, she saw God. She followed her Son right to the foot of the cross, and beyond, to the grave. Hers was a compassion. She shared his passion not only in a physical way but also in a spiritual, emotional, and deeply tragic way. 'Passionate love for mankind' and 'pain.' These two realities were like a chalice the Father had given Christ from which men would drink and know that he had forgiven them. This same chalice was given to Mary to drink. She truly compassionated — she shared the passion of her Son. She shared his passionate love for humanity, and she shared his pain. Men need other human beings, and they need, above all, gentle ones, compassionate ones. . . . (P 170-171)

Christ continues to suffer in his members, in his Body. Catherine is on her immense pilgrimage to console him, to wipe his tears. Thus, loving in this world takes on the dimension of co-suffering, or com-passion. As one ventures into the perilous land of loneliness, there is necessarily suffering. This suffering purifies the one seeking to preach Christ, joins him or her to the passion of Christ, creates compassion for the one being sought. For Catherine, love is often, in the famous phrase of Dostoyevsky, a "harsh and dreadful thing."

## Without Counting The Cost

"Without compromise," as we have seen, has the meaning of totality, passion, living the Gospel in every aspect of life and with all of one's powers and energies. Christ gave his all for us on the Cross. Such love demands our all for him.

"Without counting the cost" emphasizes that such totality, such passion, is very often painful; and that is why, of course, we tend to live mediocre lives. But real love *costs*.

In Catherine's earliest reflections on this line of the Mandate (1968) she first of all recalls words of a Jesuit priest she heard as a very young child. He was speaking about the problems of priests and how priests needed prayers. Then he said: "When you grow up perhaps some of you will offer your lives for priests." Catherine wanted to, then and there! "He looked at me over his spectacles and said: 'It will require a lot of love of a certain type. Only people who love terribly much can really offer their life.' " The most the priest would allow her to say was the following: "I, Catherine, want to offer my life for priests. I am a little girl and I am doing it as a little girl can do it. Please accept my offering." So, in Catherine's own mind and heart, offering her life for priests is one of the meanings of this line.

Another recollection which came to her was going to confession as a young girl, and the priest asking her how much she loved her enemies. "I said I didn't know I had enemies. He said: 'Maybe now you have no enemies, but you will have in the future. So always examine your conscience as to how well you love your enemies. If you love your enemies well, all is well, and you will be in the commandment of love.' " So, she says, the first two meanings she gave to this line concerned a self-offering for priests, and love of enemies.

We cannot go into her love for priests here (see *Dear Father*), but very, very deep in Catherine's soul is her life being poured out as an offering for priests. While this may have been a particular call for Catherine, her spiritual children also believe that they are called, each in his or her own way, to a special concern for the priests of the world.

In a commentary in 1969, a year later than the above reflections, she speaks more pointedly to the general meaning of the line:

I barely dare to touch upon this line of the Mandate. Speaking of myself, I have very often counted the cost. I have cried out, as Fr. Cal my spiritual director very well knows, 'Lord, that is impossible.' But Fr. Cal, I guess, helps to bring the Holy Spirit back, and I make another step towards that impossibility.

To love means to surrender to every situation, no matter how horrible and impossible. To love means to surrender to every person, no matter how obnoxious, how terrible, this person may be. It means to stand naked with the naked Christ in the marketplace for everyone to spit at you and push you around. But it also means that *it has the power to make the other surrender to God.*

Because, our love, when it is without counting the cost, is always directed towards God; then it leads people towards God. I think then our love (I wouldn't think of it as a bulldozer because I don't like machines!) is even harder to manage than a bulldozer, because it makes straight the paths of the Lord. We make straight the paths of the Lord with our bare hands and with our bare feet. Sometimes it is a path through brambles. We ourselves are torn, broken, yet we still move so that other people can follow this little path without being scratched.

It means that no matter what the price, we make a road to Christ for the other. It's in the life of the Spirit. There is no self-pity in the life of such a person who makes straight the way of the Lord. There can be no self-pity because no matter how hard it is — to love, love, love and not count the cost — there is always the Wind and the Fire; so you resolutely enter the brambles. A tremendous Wind comes in after you've made three or four steps into the brambles and whoooooosh, like a tornado, all the brambles are blown from the path.

We have to understand that we are lovers. His way is a hard way as long as I rely on myself. But it's easier when I let the Wind and the Fire carry me, following along in his footsteps. This means I must pray for *faith*. Out of this faith, which is the father of love, love grows.

Strangely enough, as we go forward, making straight the path of the Lord for others, through various and terrible circumstances (I am speaking of the domain of the soul), if we strive for the Cross, it will carry *us*. Because, strangely enough, when we follow the Fire and the Wind, when our heart is open to *his opening* of the words of the Gospel we must preach, a Shadow falls over us; and suddenly, next to us, Somebody else is walking. It's a Person. Now we are not alone any more. In the real sense of the word we are never alone; but the spittle of faith on the shadow of our substance brings Christ right next to us. In his Body, in a sense, he walks with us, though our eyes may still be held.

But as we love, and as this love grows and grows because we are opening our hearts to the Spirit, we do see, dimly, darkly, as in a mirror, some kind of Person. But there is more: we *feel* him with something that has no feeling, no sight, no touch, no smell — our *soul*.

It's strange how, as we surrender to this powerful reality of 'Love . . . love . . . love . . . never counting the cost,' you see Golgotha, you hear, 'I thirst,' and you understand Who Love is (dimly, for who can understand God?)

But now you arise. You can't help it. You must arise and go to the poor, to the rich, meaning humanity, to bring Love to them. It becomes a passion. Because you have opened your heart to the Fire and the Wind, *you are fired.* This fire in you becomes unquenchable, a hunger for the happiness of the other, which fills you.

Now nothing matters. Everybody can walk all over you until you are mush hamburger. You couldn't care less; you let them. (Well, that's an exaggeration. But in the spirit of faith, this is the ideal I give you!) Because you never forget that maybe *you have often made hamburgers of others!* That's what I always think about. So, love is a beautiful thing.   (TOLM, 1969)

Do we need any more commentary on this love? Do you see how she has summarized here almost every theme in this book? Overwhelmed by Love yourself, and aided by the Fire and the Wind (the Holy Spirit), you venture forth into the hearts of others to bring them the presence of Love. Precisely *through the pain of it all* Love walks beside you and helps to clear the bramble-cluttered path.

I believe Catherine is saying that only the pain of the Cross can reveal the Presence to us. Somehow we must break through the false self — self-absorption — to touch the Presence with our true self — the "soul." Our movement toward the other in faith and concern has the power of love to "make the other surrender to God." As our love grows, the Presence grows. And this Presence sustains us even when misunderstood, rejected — made hamburger out of! We have often rejected and misunderstood — made hamburger out of — others. Who are we to complain!

> Self-pity is one of the great boulders along our path of loving: I tried to love them but they didn't want me! Boo hoo!

> If self-pity enters in then you just plop yourself down by the side of the road and say, 'Lord, I'm not worthy of anything. I'm just a sinner. I know nothing from nothing. Choose somebody else.' Well, that's the death of the apostolate. Why don't we all acknowledge right here and now, in one voice, 'I am a sinner. I am a failure.' (*Ibid.*)

Self-pity will block our path into the hearts of others if we rely on ourselves instead of God, if we take our eyes off Love.

## Pain Is the Kiss Of Christ

Catherine had a wooden plaque in her cabin with this saying on it, "Pain is the kiss of Christ"; we all saw it many, many times, and heard her say this many times. She often reminded us that pain is part of life, one of life's great teachers, and yes, one of life's great benefactors. (And, if we are faithful enough to love, it could even become the kiss of Christ.) Perhaps there are many depths of being and knowledge we will never attain except through suffering. To try and avoid all pain is totally against the Christian understanding of life.

> Christ defined all the ways of loving — not only defined them, lived them. He was Love Incarnate, and he showed us that in truth *greater love has no man than to lay down his life for his brethren* — accentuating that love has no limits.
>
> Perhaps this is why there is so much talk about love, so much experimenting — and so much disappointment with what we imagine love to be. Because deep down in our hearts we know that his way of loving is the way of the Cross, that it is painful, and that it demands an emptying of ourselves. None of us can love the way he wants us to love him.
>
> True. All this spells pain to us moderns who take sleeping pills and traquilizers by the ton to alleviate the slightest anxiety and pain. But if we arise and follow his road of love we shall know joy beyond all telling. Incredible as it may seem, if we follow that road of love which Christ etched out for us we will solve most of our modern problems.   (R, Sept., 1968)

We have lost our faith in the power of redemptive, suffering love. Sitting with someone in his or her pain (as one of our guests expressed it once, "When I can no longer sit with myself") loving them, being present to them with the love of Christ in our hearts — these kind of acts will produce more fruit than all the programs and sophisticated approaches to "helping people." What people need most of all is someone to enter their "land of loneliness" and help them to see the Presence with their own eyes:

> Words like 'production,' 'efficiency,' 'competence,' are constantly bandied about at various meetings and conferences of lay apostolic groups in this land. But we have been created in the image and likeness of God. Our value, the yardstick of our worth, is the Incarnation of God who was, is, man. Perhaps we could say that our value is the three hours he spent on the cross, dying out of love for us.
>
> It seems, at times, that these three hours were really very 'inefficient,' 'incompetent,' 'unproductive,' — actually a failure in the eyes of men. His death must have appeared, even to the apostles, as the acme of uselessness. They expected something more efficient, more competent, more productive. Instead, there was that seemingly useless death!
>
> They hadn't experienced Pentecost yet. We have. But we still seem to forget that love cannot be measured in human terms, cannot be analyzed in laboratories, cannot be measured in terms of efficiency and understood by the world.
>
> Love is a spendthrift. It doesn't mind wasting time in listening to someone in pain, or visiting some shabby street, or doing nothing more than smile at some unsmiling faces. A year or two later — quite inefficient! — one of those faces may smile back!   (R, May, 1967)
>
> The price of souls is high — as high as the cross on which we must hang. Unless we do so there will be no success, because we do not love enough . . . because passionate love, the love that leads to Golgotha, has not yet begun to consume us. . . .   (SL #117, 1962)

# NOTE ON THE THIRD VOLUME:
## A Preview

[ * * * ]

IN THE THIRD VOLUME of this series, which will discuss the last three lines of the Mandate, we will see how the journey to the lonely Christ is progressively revealed as a pilgrimage into the human heart. The "marketplace" of the sixth line is the human heart, where all the buying and selling takes place, where all the idols are, and out of which, the Lord tells us, proceeds murder, hatred, adultery, and all the evils of the human race. We are told not to be afraid to enter there — "Go without fears into the depths of men's hearts" — for the Lord will be with us. He will be not only with us but in us, and we will bring his Presence into that place which needs his life and light.

Prayer and fasting — "Pray . . . fast" — are the two powerful spiritual weapons we must use to not only be able to enter but to withstand the "demons" within. There will always be people who do not know and love the Lord. So, one can never rest in this life without zeal for the neighbor's salvation. In this life we can only "rest" in the midst of the human condition. It is a paradoxical rest, at one and the same time in the depth of the market-place and in the depth of God.

Catherine once received a beautiful word from the Lord. It was to the effect that every human heart is filled with a precious perfume. But this flask must be broken open so that the perfume can be poured out on the feet of the Lord. The painful Cross is the breaking open of this flask. But it is only so that the beautiful perfume — the "odor of Christ" within us — can be poured forth on the feet of others, which are the feet of Christ.

You might say that the last three lines of the Mandate are about how to "get into" the human heart. It is the most impregnable of all fortresses on earth. Even God himself cannot "get in" if the heart is not opened from within. The Little Mandate of Catherine is a wonderful, elaborate, delicate, intricate "strategy of love," coaxing, enticing, wooing the human heart to open from within, like a flower, so that we can enter there with great delicacy, and reveal the overwhelming love of Christ, reveal Christ himself Who is Love.

# APPENDIX

[ * * * ]

*Letter No. 76*
*June 20, 1962*

*Dearly Beloved:*

*Some time ago the whole house had a long discussion. We gathered in Eddie's\* room, and the conversation drifted to the big topic of* little things. *So here is a staff letter coming to you to remind you again of the little things that are so important.*

*The first thought that comes to me as foundress of this place is: for reasons that I will never fathom (since it is a mystery of God until I see him), he touched me and said, "Comes."*

*You have often read how I discuss my vocation as a stupendous adventure. Let's begin with that. I was just breathless when God called me. Thirty years later, I am just as breathless as on that first day when I realized that this vocation had come to me.*

---

\* Edward Doherty:   Catherine's husband.

*Okay, now get the picture of a young woman realizing that God has gloriously called her, although at the time she was responsible for a child, and a lot of other things. One gift that I have had since childhood is a great faith. Faith is a gift from God. You can pray for it, but you can't grow in faith unless he gives you the grace. It is a free gift from God. Knowing what he was going to do with me, he endowed me with a very strong faith.*

*Now as I look back, and as I look at you, I think maybe you, if you were a married woman without a husband, and with a child, would have hesitated. If a call like that had come to you, you might have hesitated because you are Americans and Canadians, having a lot of possessions. I don't know. Maybe you would have done what I did and just said, "God, I don't understand. Now it is up to you to remove the obstacles."*

*So he removed them through a bishop.*

*Then, when I received the permission, I took the plunge. That is, I took my son and "yanked myself" into the slums. I consider this one of the "little things" because I keep repeating to you this poem: "Lord, I throw at your feet my life and sing that I give you such a little thing."*

*For there before my eyes is a crucifix — to me, living, breathing, full of wounds, and saying to me, "I love you, I love you." When I compare my life with that crucifix, then my whole life is nothing. So to begin with, I consider that the gift of my whole life from the day that he called me to the day that I am speaking to you, is a tiny little thing in proportion to what he gave me.*

*Now, is that clear — what I call a "little thing"? I think that we misunderstood each other right here. Understand that, for me, my whole life is as nothing to give — I wish that I had a thousand lives to give him. Then you will understand why I consider it to be a "little thing."*

*Now if I consider that my life is about as big as a thimble, then what is in it is still smaller, isn't it? "I sing and sing that I throw at your feet my life — such a small thing." If I consider that my life which I throw at God's feet is such a small thing, then what is inside cannot be bigger than the whole, can it?*

*I am a poor woman. I wrote a poem. You don't read my poems much, and probably they don't mean too much to you, for the language is symbolic, but some day you might understand them. I wrote a poem one day in which I said:*

> I am nothing
> A beggar
> Covered with wounds
> Lying upon
> A thousand roads. . . .

*Meaning that I am nothing, that I am the least of all, and that I can't offer him anything. But he touched me.*

> But you came
> My king,
> And touched me
> With your hand,
> And I arose
> And I followed you. . . .

*He touched me — a dirty, unwashed, no-good soul. I am not deprecating myself; I am a marvelous creature. I have been created in the image and likeness of God. But we are all sinners,* and when I say that I consider myself a sinner, I mean it!

*So, what can a grain of sand, who is a sinner, do for God? Little things. I am in Friendship House. Everyone in the place is calling me names. Priests do not believe in what I am doing. Only one lonely bishop and two spiritual directors believe in me. Day-in and day-out, hour-in and hour-out, I hear, "Look at that woman! She probably sleeps with those hoboes."*

*But I consider this persecution a "little thing." It is the tiniest of little things to be persecuted for twenty-one years out of thirty. I consider it very little to offer to God!*

*So I talk of little things. Probably to you persecution would be something very big. I am so small, so unworthy. I have only one life to throw at his feet, and it is so* small. *He gave me his* life. *And he is God.*

*So I ask, what can a little person do who tries to love God tremendously? And I answer, everything: from putting the lights off because of holy poverty, to refraining from changing clothes every five minutes because there is a clothing room, to being indifferent to food, to going where God calls you.*

*Now here again, let us understand one another, for I do not think that we do. First, remember that I have a personal relationship with Christ. To me he is real; is in this room. Besides my faith, I have a vivid imagination. He is* real.

*So, there is a knock at the door. Someone calls for my nursing services. No matter how tired and exhausted I am,* I know that it is God knocking! I literally see his hand with a wound. *(I don't mean in a vision, but in my imagination.)*

*You pass by and whisper, "B, may I see you today?" So unless something more important intervenes, something that he also wants, I will talk with you.*

*My day is directed simply by the needs of the Apostolate. I weigh those needs. Should I dictate three hours or four? For you it is simpler, and I envy you! You know his will. You know it clearly every second of the day. How lucky you are! I have to make decisions. Fortunately, if I am confused, I have Father Cal to tell me what to choose.*

*But once I know God's will I am going to try to do it perfectly. My heart swells and I say, "This also, Lord, for love of you." I know very well its redemptive value. Do I speak too symbolically?*

*Another example: I have empty hands. At night I consider that I have to bring something to the altar for tomorrow's paten. What can I bring? I can bring a thousand buttons well-sorted with great love, understanding full well that because of my attention these buttons have redemptive value. I can bring hours of conversation with you. I can bring many letters with attention to details.*

*This faith comes from a tremendous, personal understanding that God is* real, *and* my tremendous Lover. *He has first given his life for me. In the face of that gift I am like one who is bereft of my senses! I go around gathering every flower so that I can bring it to him. It is his will that directs the gathering.*

*In March I shall speak to the Medical Association — the psychiatrists — and I'll be a "big shot," quote unquote. They will meet me at the train; they'll make a fuss over me. They'll put me up at the biggest hotel. "This is the great Baroness de Hueck, the celebrated lecturer of the United States, the author of books — " Now to me all of this is exactly the same as doing the buttons! There is no difference.*

*Writing these books, is a little thing for me. You read my books; they have been written piecemeal. I have never said to myself, "Now I will write a book." I would only do so if Father told me: "I want you to take three hours every day and write a book." Then, I would try to write a book. But I don't need three hours to write a book. Why don't I need three hours? Because I write what I live. I don't need any solitude, reference books or anything else. I write only what I live. I couldn't write a story, plot, an essay, if you paid me!*

*Why do I write as I do? Because I love. It is so simple. Any one of you could write to your girlfriends about your boyfriends. You went out with your boyfriend and you are writing your best friend about Joe. You become eloquent, because you love Joe! And you, who ordinarily cannot put two words together, will write or scribble six pages to your girlfriend about Joe!*

*So that's what I do. It's so simple. That's what I want you to do. Yes, even writing books is a little thing.*

*So to me, life is all little things. Thoughtfulness. Fr. Cal says to me, "Katie, I don't want you to talk to anybody in the morning; you have low-blood pressure and you feel, shall we say, a little upset." Then I try not to talk in the morning. I obey him. If I disobey him, I go to confession.*

*But sometimes this combination of tension and low-blood pressure in me creates a quick retort. Well, then I am really sad, because I feel that this is a "big thing." Sin is a big thing. Anything connected with sin is a big thing, because it hurts love. Everything else is very small.*

*It never occurs to me that you can possibly separate any- thing from love. That is why I keep pushing the priests, almost impolitely, to connect daily life with poverty and reverence. I have no right to do that, but I do so unconsciously. The words are out before I can control them. I must work on that. As I told you, I am a sinner!*

*For example, I will speak of cups, because you seem to have an aversion to washing dishes. If you have this attitude that this is a beautiful, little thing that you can give to God, then washing a cup becomes an adventure. It is this sense of adventure, glory, and joy that you lack.*

*I have lots of fun. I might be terribly tired, and the job might be monotonous but I will make it interesting for myself. For example, many of you saw the terrible monotony of the library work down in the basement before Christmas. You saw that I was sometimes tense, and sometimes, perhaps, a bit sharp, for which I was sorry. Nevertheless, I kept thinking, "Gee, this is wonderful! Generations of our members are going to benefit from this." Again a little thing to give to God. Now, do you get the picture, or are you still missing the point of what I mean by "little things"? The whole of life is a "little thing" which we throw at God's feet and sing and sing. Every little thing should be done perfectly, completely connected with God, for otherwise, it ceases to be interesting. It has no sense and no being.*

*There is great freedom in this. You don't have to "smile" doing the little things. The very fact that, in your hearts you enjoy doing them will radiate in your eyes, will show forth in your concentration.*

*People come here for summer school.\* Why do you think that they come here? They come to see human beings throw their lives at Christ's feet and sing that they bring him such a small thing. They touch us, and then change in some way, or receive graces from Christ.*

*This is your Apostolate. If you go to Marian Centre, and wash dishes, the whole of Edmonton is changed. For Edmonton is changed in quite a big way because Marian Centre is there.*

---

\* Madonna House formerly had a summer school of Catholic Action.

*Whitehorse, Yukon is changed because of the presence of Maryhouse! By doing those little things you radiate love, and that is the Apostolate.*

*Both the talented ones and those who have no particular talents all contribute to the restoration of the world to Christ.* It is not what you do that matters. It is what you are. *If you have understood the romance and immensity of "little things," then you will restore the world to Christ. You will be an adventuresome, joyous, glad, simple, and humble light by doing little things. They will become big because they are touched by God and done for him.*

*Now, have I explained what the "little things" are, or are you still confused? How is it possible to live this life as a vocation, unless you connect every gesture and breath with God? Unless you have an awareness of every lamp that is lit unnecessarily? Unless you pick up everything after everybody, and after yourself, especially, so as not to burden your brother? Unless you are completely* in every little thing *with your whole heart, your whole soul, your whole mind, this is not the vocation for you. Go elsewhere, but wherever you go you will certainly have to do little things. Try to do them without love, and see what happens. But doing little things with our whole heart is our vocation.*

*Maybe sometime you will be a great professor in a university. But then, you will be utterly indifferent to being a professor. You must neither refuse anything to God, nor ask anything as far as your vocation is concerned.*

*Christ is a piece of bread that the priest carries, and you too, are a piece of bread that is carried on the wind and word of your superiors. You are another Christ, glad to go anywhere, and glad to do anything, always considering everything so very small, because what he gives you is so very big.*

*The smallness is always in relation to God, but the hunger to return to God is immense. The only "big thing" about you is your hunger to love — to be and to do — for God.*

*Is that clear? It's so simple! Of course we must also do "little things" well in our personal relationships. How else are we going to learn to love unless we love one another? What is the use of going to learn to love unless we love one another? What is the use of preaching and talking about Christ, unless we are Christ to one another?*

*It all hinges on God as Person, on the sense of adventure, the sense of call and on the three lines of this poem: "Lord, I throw at your feet my life, and sing and sing that I give you such a small thing."*

*That's all. Once you get that picture, you've got the whole thing. It's possible that you might not be called to this life. However, once you are in it, then you know that you are called. Then, it is your vocation, and you have to accept and act accordingly. You cannot just connect a "little" with God; you must connect completely.*

*But if you are not connecting completely, go and seek help. It can happen. Emotional or other kinds of problems might sometimes obscure the realization of your vocation. Turn to God and seek help from God, and from those who can give it to you. You have the vocation. This means that you must live the life sooner or later. That's what I mean by "little things."*

*There is also the cross. I should speak about that also. I cannot visualize a love story with God without a cross. To me, the cross is the thing! I desire it, I accept it, and I ask the grace never to fear it, because one day I shall know its joy.*

*You may think that I am just talking through my hat. But again, as God is my witness, I look at the cross as the marriage bed of Christ. I desire union with him at the price of being crucified. Then my soul cries out, "Where are the nails? Where is the hammer?" Even though my flesh flinches. Of course the cross is there. When I talk about the cross I think that you misunderstand what I mean. For me the cross is the key to him whom my heart loves. Without the cross, there is no Easter. Unless I lie on my cross, I can't see him in heaven. But I must lie on the cross that* he *made for me, not the one* I'm *making for myself.*

*This is all so clear to me that I, quite naturally, talk to you about the cross. However, I am beginning to think that for you the cross is something heavy. Something that you wish you could throw off, something that you have to carry, but you do so without joy.*

*God embraced the cross because he wanted to. For this he was born! For this we are born — to lie on it with him. I literally mean the words that I say, but I don't think that you understand me. That's why you have a problem with "little things."*

*Does that make sense to you? Do you understand how I think and feel about these things? You may disagree with it or not understand it, but this is what I mean by "little things." If you wish to be in this Apostolate, you have to come to this understanding with the help of the priests and myself, and afterwards through my writings. For this is your vocation. This is what he gave me. I'm passing it on to you.*

*When somebody says to me, "Catherine, I don't think that I can take a lifetime of these little things. It's excruciating." I want to weep. It's a failure to understand our* faith. *The same person, whoever he or she is, will have a lifetime of other little things that will be just as excruciating.*

*However, never think of your vocation as a lot of monotonous "little things."*

*Think of it as the glory of the cross. Measure the "little things" against* his bigness — what he has done for us. *Try every minute to put a little grain of sand before the altar, and before you die, you might have a mountain to offer. It is so simple!*

Lovingly in Mary,

Catherine

# KEY TO CITED WORKS

[ * * * ]

So as not to get complicated, I have devised a simple key to Catherine's writings. Sometimes I am working from the published editions; then I will quote the page reference. Sometimes I am working from original manuscripts; in that case I simply quote the work, since the public does not have access to the reference anyhow. I will list here also works of Catherine not used in this book so as to give the reader an overall view of her published, and some of her unpublished writings.

   AF - *Apostolic Farming*. Private printing.
    CI - "The Church and I." Unpublished talk.
 COLM - "Comments on the Little Mandate." Unpublished talk, 1967.
   DB - *Dear Bishop* (New York: Sheed and Ward, 1947).
   DF - *Dear Father* (New York: Alba House, 1978).
  DLR - *Doubts, Loneliness, Rejection* (New York: Alba House, 1981).
  DSem - *Dear Seminarian* (Milwaukee: Bruce Publishing Company, 1950).
  DSis - *Dear Sister* (Milwaukee: Bruce Publishing Company, 1953).
   FH - *Friendship House* (New York: Sheed and Ward, 1946).
   FL - Furfey Letters. Catherine's correspondence with her former spiritual director, Fr. Paul Furfey, when she was in Harlem.
  FML - *Fragments of My Life* (Notre Dame, IN: Ave Maria Press, 1979).
  GPW - *The Gospel of A Poor Woman* (Denville, NJ: Dimension Books, 1981).
  GWC - *The Gospel Without Compromise* (Notre Dame, IN: Ave Maria Press, 1976).

HA - *The History of the Apostolate.* 3 Vols. Unpublished. Catherine's personal account of the history of her apostolate, starting in Toronto, then continuing in Harlem and Combermere.

HMCB - "How the Little Mandate Came To Be." Unpublished talk, 1968.

ILI - *I Live On An Island* (Notre Dame, IN: Ave Maria Press, 1979).

JI, I & II - *Journey Inward.* Two volumes of Catherine's poetry privately published here at Madonna House. I refer to it either as JI, I or JI, II. Some of these poems have been published. See next reference, *Lubov*, and *My Heart and I.*

JI - *Journey Inward* (New York: Alba House, 1984).

LDM - "Local Directors' Meetings." Unpublished. These were talks given at our yearly meetings here at Madonna House.

L - *Lubov* (Locust Valley, New York: Living Flame Press, 1985). Some of her poetry.

M - *Molchanie* (New York: Crossroad Publishing Co., 1982).

MHI - *My Heart and I* (Petersham, MA: St. Bede's Publications, 1987). Poetry.

MHWII - *Madonna House, What Is It?* Unpublished manuscript, 1980.

MRY - *My Russian Yesterdays* (Milwaukee: Bruce Publishing Company, 1951).

NWP - *Not Without Parables* (Notre Dame, IN: Ave Maria Press, 1977).

OC - *Out of the Crucible.* Some Ideas On Training For the Lay Apostolate. (New York: St. Paul's Publications, 1961).

OLUM - *Our Lady's Unknown Mysteries* (Denville, NJ: Dimension Books, 1979).

P - *Poustinia* (Notre Dame, IN: Ave Maria Press, 1975). Catherine's classic, now in over six languages.

Pov - *Poverty.* Unpublished manuscript. Catherine's final, comprehensive statement on this aspect of the Gospel, 1980.

PTW - *The People of the Towel and the Water* (Denville, NJ: Dimension Books, 1978). Her best description of the Madonna House way of life.

R - *Restoration.* The monthly newspaper of Madonna House. (Only $3.00 a year!)

SC - *Stations of the Cross.* A Meditation. Private printing, 1954.

SL - *Staff Letters.* Unpublished letters of Catherine to her community of Madonna House. Vol. I available from Madonna House gift shop.

SLFF - *Staff Letters From the Foundress.* A new series of the above, beginning in 1970.

SMHA - "The Spirit of the Madonna House Apostolate." A talk given in 1956. Printed in JLC.

SMS - *Soul of My Soul.* Reflections From a Life of Prayer (Notre Dame, IN: Ave Maria Press, 1985).

So - *Sobornost* (Notre Dame, IN: Ave Maria Press, 1977).

St - *Strannik* (Notre Dame Press, IN: Ave Maria Press, 1978).

TOLM - "Thoughts on the Little Mandate." Unpublished talk given at the Directors' Meeting, 1969.

U - *Urodivoi,* Fools For God (New York: Crossroad Publishing Co., 1983).

WL - "Way of Life." The official Constitution of Madonna House written by Catherine, 1970-71.

WLIGI - *Where Love Is, God Is* (Milwaukee: Bruce Publishing Co., 1953).

# OTHER WORKS

AIHLY - *As I Have Loved You* (Dublin, Ireland: Veritas Publications, 1988). The Life of Catherine de Hueck Doherty. Omer Tanghe.

JLC - *Journey To Lonely Christ.* The "Little Mandate" of Catherine de Hueck Doherty (New York: Alba House, 1987). Robert Wild. This is the first volume of my trilogy on the Mandate.

T - *Tumbleweed* (Milwaukee: Bruce Publishing Company, 1948). Life of Catherine by her late husband, Eddie Doherty.

## An Interesting Thought

The publication you have just finished reading is part of the apostolic efforts of the Society of St. Paul of the American Province. The Society of St. Paul is an international religious community located in 23 countries, whose particular call and ministry is to bring the message of Christ to all people through the communications media.

Following in the footsteps of their patron, St. Paul the Apostle, priests and brothers blend a life of prayer and technology as writers, editors, marketing directors, graphic designers, bookstore managers, pressmen, sound engineers, etc. in the various fields of the mass media, to announce the message of Jesus.

If you know a young man who might be interested in a religious vocation as a brother or priest and who shows talent and skill in the communications arts, ask him to consider our life and ministry. For more information at no cost or obligation write:

**Vocation Office**
2187 Victory Blvd.
Staten Island, NY 10314-6603
Telephone: (718) 698-3698